GRM
ISRAELI BIBLE SCHOOL

GLOBAL REVIVAL MESSIANIC, APOSTOLIC, PROPHETIC BIBLE SCHOOL

STUDENT WORKBOOK
LEVELS 1-3

© 2023 by Dominiquae Bierman
GRM Israeli Bible School: Student Workbook by Dominiquae Bierman

All rights reserved. This book may not be copied or reprinted for commercial gain or profit. Using short quotations or occasional page copying for personal or group study is permitted and encouraged. We will grant permission upon request.

Unless otherwise identified, all scripture quotations are from the Tree of Life Version (TLV) and the New American Standard Bible (NASB). Tree of Life Version. © 2015 by the Messianic Jewish Family Bible Society. Used by permission of the Messianic Jewish Family Bible Society. New American Standard Bible. © 1995 by the Lockman Foundation. Used by permission, all rights reserved.

Words such as Jesus, Christ, Lord, and God have been changed by the author back to their original Hebrew renderings, Yeshua, Yahveh, and Elohim.

Paperback ISBN: 978-1-953502-75-9

First paperback edition March 2023
Published by Zion's Gospel Press
shalom@zionsgospel.com
52 Tuscan Way, Ste 202-412,
St. Augustine, Florida 32092, USA

First Printed March 2023
Published in the United States of America

ZIONS GOSPEL
PRESS

GRM BIBLE SCHOOL

PREPARE FOR A JOURNEY OF LIFE-CHANGING DISCOVERY...

Dearly Beloved,

First of all, we would like to thank you for being courageous enough to start this remarkable journey of restoration. It takes a real heart of zeal to seek the Kingdom of God in its fullest, and we can attest that during this course, you will develop Godly understanding and your faith will grow remarkably. By the end of this course, you will be prepared to tackle some of the hardest questions concerning the Hebrew and Jewish roots of the faith.

This course is a preliminary foundation required to unlearn the lies which have been spread for centuries—concerning the Jewishness of the Gospel and Messiah. After the course is when the application of what you've learned kicks in. May you be blessed as you come in and out of this course. We look forward to your testimonies of freedom and experience!

HOW TO USE THE WORKBOOK

Please read these instructions to be well-informed on how to complete GRM Bible School. This workbook is vital during the study of GRM Bible School Levels 1-3. This workbook is divided into three levels, with units containing lessons.

Depending on study type, watch video lessons online, by DVD, or within a study group.

At the end of each lesson, there is a set of Quizzes. Answer them by choosing an option. You can check your answers at the end of the Quizzes in that Lesson. You will also have to write a Term Paper after each of the 3 Levels. There will be an instructor, a "Marker" to approve your work. Make a word document/written paper with answers to the questions and submit it to the Marker.

After the Quizzes for every Level, you will also find the reading schedule, and the Quizzes for the books.

Appendix A at the back of this workbook includes a list of the 10 Commandments with other laws and commandments of God.

GRM Israeli Bible School uses several types of materials:

- Books
- The Bible
- The Internet
- The Student Workbook
- Videos

Please take some time to familiarize these materials, especially the workbook: This workbook is the connection with everything.

LESSONS

Each lesson in this workbook has a corresponding video lesson.

SUBMITTING STUDENT WORK

Students need to submit the Term Papers. Work will be reviewed, commented on, and then returned.

How do I submit my work for correction?

All work will be submitted by email unless otherwise instructed. When sending work through an email to the Marker, submit as an attachment. Do not send attachments in-line as part of the email, but only as an attachment.

What format should I use for my work?

Microsoft Word Documents (.DOCX) is the preferred format for submitting work. Other formats are not always readable on the computer of a Marker.

What do I need to include with my work?

Everything you submit must have the following information on the document:

Your Name, Student ID, Level Number, and Term Paper.

Format is double spaced with size 12 font.

GRM BIBLE SCHOOL

WORKBOOK TABLE OF CONTENTS

Contents

LEVEL 1: FOUNDATIONS OF FAITH REVEALED 1

UNIT 1 3

    Lesson 1 5

    Lesson 2 7

    Lesson 3 9

    Lesson 4 11

    Lesson 5 13

    Lesson 6 15

UNIT 2 17

    Lesson 7 19

    Lesson 8 21

UNIT 3 23

    Lesson 9 25

    Lesson 10 27

UNIT 4 29

    Lesson 11 31

    Lesson 12 33

    Lesson 13 35

    Lesson 14 37

    Lesson 15 39

UNIT 5 41

    Lesson 16 43

    Lesson 17 45

Lesson 18 47

Unit 6 49

Lesson 19 51

Lesson 20 53

Lesson 21 55

Lesson 22 57

Lesson 23 59

Lesson 24 61

Lesson 25 63

Unit 7 65

Lesson 26 67

Lesson 27 69

Lesson 28 71

Unit 8 73

Lesson 29 75

Lesson 30 77

Lesson 31 79

Lesson 32 81

Lesson 33 83

Reading Schedule 85

Healing Power of the Roots 85

Grafted In 89

Sheep Nations 91

Vision Negev 93

Term Paper 95

LEVEL 2: DISCOVERING THE HEBREW SCRIPTURES 97

Unit 9 99

Lesson 34 101

Lesson 35 103

Lesson 36	105
Lesson 37	107
Lesson 38	109
Lesson 39	111
Lesson 40	113
Lesson 41	115

UNIT 10 117

Lesson 42	119
Lesson 43	121
Lesson 44	123
Lesson 45	125
Lesson 46	127
Lesson 47	129

UNIT 11 131

Lesson 48	133
Lesson 49	135

UNIT 12 137

Lesson 50	139
Lesson 51	141
Lesson 52	143
Lesson 53	145
Lesson 54	147
Lesson 55	149

READING SCHEDULE 151

Yeshua Is The Name	151
Stormy Weather	155
Eradicating the Cancer of Religion	157
Restoration of the Holy Giving	159

TERM PAPER 161

LEVEL 3: HEBREW SCRIPTURES RESTORED 163

Unit 13 165
- Lesson 56 167
- Lesson 57 169
- Lesson 58 171
- Lesson 59 173
- Lesson 60 175
- Lesson 61 177
- Lesson 62 179
- Lesson 63 181

Unit 14 183
- Lesson 64 185
- Lesson 65 187
- Lesson 66 189
- Lesson 67 191

Unit 15 193
- Lesson 68 195
- Lesson 69 197
- Lesson 70 199

Unit 16 201
- Lesson 71 203
- Lesson 72 205
- Lesson 73 207

Unit 17 209
- Lesson 74 211
- Lesson 75 213

Unit 18 215
- Lesson 76 217
- Lesson 77 219

 Lesson 78 221

 Lesson 79 223

UNIT 19 225

 Lesson 80 227

 Lesson 81 229

READING SCHEDULE 231

 The Key of Abraham 231

 The MAP Revolution 235

 The Bible Cure for Africa and the Nations 237

 The Woman Factor 239

TERM PAPER 241

APPENDIX A – THE TEN COMMANDMENTS 243

APPENDIX B: FOR FURTHER STUDIES 245

APPENDIX C: GRADUATION & ORDINATION 245

GRM ISRAELI BIBLE SCHOOL
LEVEL 1: FOUNDATIONS OF FAITH REVEALED

STUDENT WORKBOOK
UNITS 1-8

www.grmbibleschool.com

info@grmbibleschool.com

GRM BIBLE SCHOOL

Israel Rediscovered

Unit 1

GRM BIBLE SCHOOL

WELCOME PROGRAM

UNIT 1

Lesson 1 – Return

1. The Hebrew word "Teshuva" means to _____, to repent and be restored.
    a. Stop
    b. Awaken
    c. Return
    d. Be saved

2. The Hebrew foundations of faith were lost through the Council of _____ in 325 C.E
    a. Trent
    b. Nicaea
    c. Laodicea
    d. Jerusalem

3. Constantine established Christianity as the official religion of the Roman Empire and included many _____ traditions.
    a. Religious
    b. Sacred
    c. Bloody
    d. Pagan

4. After returning to God we must return to His _____.
    a. People
    b. Torah
    c. Land of Israel
    d. None of the above

5. The Key of _____ brings revival and covenant blessings even during times of great judgment.
    a. David
    b. Yeshua
    c. Abraham
    d. Moses

6. We need to rediscover the original Hebrew foundations of faith as handed to the Jewish Apostles by

_____ to be given to the nations.
   a. Yeshua
   b. Paul
   c. Timothy
   d. None of the above

7. Through GRM Bible School, we will learn how to restore the relationship between _____ and the Church.
   a. Pagans
   b. Jews
   c. Catholics
   d. Government

ANSWERS

1. c
2. b
3. d
4. b
5. c
6. a
7. b

GRM BIBLE SCHOOL

ISRAEL REDISCOVERED

UNIT 1

PART 1

Lesson 2 – Restoration of Israel

1. The history of Israel begins through the Patriarch _____
    a. Moses
    b. Abraham
    c. Jacob
    d. Noah

2. The Gospel is written all over the land of _____.
    a. Goshen
    b. Syria
    c. Israel
    d. Egypt

3. God is still keeping His _____.
    a. Word
    b. Covenant
    c. Promises
    d. All of the above

4. The Jordan River in Hebrew means the river that _____.
    a. Descends
    b. Runs deep
    c. Flows swiftly
    d. Overflows

5. God said to Abraham: In you all the families of the _____ will be blessed.
    a. Earth
    b. Desert
    c. Negev
    d. Israelites

6. Zechariah 2:8; "Whoever touches Israel touches the _____ of My eye."
    a. Focus
    b. Desire
    c. Lid
    d. Apple

7. The Covenant is everlasting, forever, to _____ generations
    a. A thousand
    b. Many
    c. All
    d. None of the above

ANSWERS

1. b
2. c
3. d
4. a
5. a
6. d
7. a

GRM BIBLE SCHOOL

ISRAEL REDISCOVERED

UNIT 1

PART 2

Lesson 3 – Importance of Jerusalem

1. Jerusalem is the place of God's _____ on the earth.
   a. Eye
   b. Rulership
   c. Rest
   d. Identity

2. Psalm 122:6; "Pray for the _____ of Jerusalem."
   a. Peace
   b. Shalom (completeness, wellbeing)
   c. Undivided city
   d. All of the above

3. The plan of the enemy is to make sure Jerusalem is divided and fragmented, so it cannot be prepared for
   a. The coming of Messiah
   b. Defending itself
   c. More people making aliyah
   d. Understanding the Torah

4. From the womb of Jerusalem came forth
   a. The true gospel made in Zion
   b. The Jewish Messiah
   c. The Ten Commandments
   d. A & B above

5. Isaiah 62:6 & 7 reminds us to be watchmen "And give Him no rest until He establishes and makes Jerusalem a _____ in the earth".
   a. Superpower
   b. Gem
   c. Praise
   d. Watchtower

6. Zechariah 14:4 states that when Yeshua returns He will plant His feet on the Mount of _____ in Jerusalem.
    a. Transfiguration
    b. Olives
    c. Beatitudes
    d. Sinai

7. "Jerusalem will be a cup that causes _____ to all peoples" (Zech. 12:2)
    a. Destruction
    b. Blessings
    c. Trembling
    d. Joyfulness

ANSWERS

1. b
2. d
3. a
4. d
5. c
6. b
7. c

GRM BIBLE SCHOOL

ISRAEL REDISCOVERED

UNIT 1

PART 3

Lesson 4 – Temple Mount

1. The Temple Mount has always been contested, as holding this property gives _____ over the nations.
    a. Power
    b. Prestige
    c. Financial gains
    d. Religious control

2. _____ destroyed the Temple in the year 70 C.E.
    a. Assyrians
    b. Greeks
    c. Romans
    d. Egyptians

3. Jerusalem and the Temple Mount are _____ mentioned in the Quran.
    a. Consistently
    b. Often
    c. Never
    d. None of the above

4. _____ built the first Temple. After Ezra and Nehemiah, the second Temple was built.
    a. Abraham
    b. Solomon
    c. Herod
    d. Agrippa

5. According to 2nd Samuel 7:13, God will establish His _____ forever on the Temple Mount
    a. Name
    b. Word
    c. People
    d. Throne

6. During the 1967 Six-Day War, Israel captured the Temple Mount from Jordan and the flag of Israel waved over the Temple Mount. It was the first time in 2,000 years that Jews could pray at the Western Wall which is called the _____.
   a. House of Prayer
   b. Golden Gate
   c. Glory of Zion
   d. Kotel

7. _____ washed themselves before entering the Temple in a mikvah, which is a ritual pool or bath.
   a. Pilgrims
   b. Priests
   c. Musicians
   d. A & B

ANSWERS

1. a
2. c
3. c
4. b
5. d
6. d
7. b

GRM BIBLE SCHOOL

ISRAEL REDISCOVERED

UNIT 1

PART 4

Lesson 5 – Judgment By Storm

1. God uses storms as judgment against those who come against _____.
    a. Christians
    b. Israel
    c. United States
    d. Muslim

2. True or False: When nations come against Israel they come against God Himself.
    a. True
    b. False

3. Hurricane Katrina hit the United States immediately after the _____ were expelled from their homes and removed from Gaza in August 2005.
    a. Jews
    b. Muslims
    c. Christians
    d. None of the above

4. As long as God is speaking we have hope to _____, but, when God becomes silent, there is no more hope.
    a. Prosper
    b. Rejoice
    c. Awaken
    d. Repent

5. Psalm 83 describes an evil plan: "Come and let us wipe them out as a nation, that the name of _____ be remembered no more."
    a. Israel
    b. Yahveh
    c. Abraham
    d. Yeshua

6. He makes the _____ His messengers, flames of fire His servants. (ref. Psalm 104:4)
   a. Nations
   b. Winds
   c. Enemies
   d. Angels

7. Within 24-hours after U.S. leaders come against God's plan for Israel terrible _____ hit the United States.
   a. Debt
   b. Murders
   c. Storms
   d. Attacks

ANSWERS

1. b
2. a
3. a
4. d
5. a
6. b
7. c

GRM BIBLE SCHOOL

ISRAEL REDISCOVERED

UNIT 1

PART 5

Lesson 6 – Spiritual Aliyah

---

1. When a Jew Immigrates to Israel he makes _____.
    a. Pilgrimage
    b. Aliyah
    c. Alignment
    d. Covenant

2. Aliyah means "to go up to _____".
    a. Yah (God)
    b. Jerusalem
    c. Heaven
    d. Mt. Sinai

3. God is calling both Jew and Gentile to make Spiritual Ascension or Spiritual _____
    a. Conversion
    b. Aliyah
    c. Commitment
    d. Enlightenment

4. God is calling His people, for every Christian to be grafted into the Olive Tree that is _____. (Romans 11:17-24)
    a. Fruitful
    b. Jerusalem
    c. Israel
    d. Blooming

5. "In those days ten men from all languages and nations will take firm hold of one Jew by the hem of his robe and say, 'Let us go with you, because we have heard that _____ is with you.' (Zech. 8:23)
    a. Blessing
    b. Peace
    c. Joy

d. Yah (God)

6. Isaiah 2:3 says, "Come, let us go up (Aliyah) to the mountain of Yah , to the house of the God of _____. He will teach us His ways, so that we may walk in His paths."
   a. David
   b. Isaac
   c. Abraham
   d. Jacob

7. True or False: The prayer of King Solomon in 2nd Chronicles 6:32-33 excluded all foreigners to partake of the blessings of Yah.
   a. True
   b. False

ANSWERS

1. b
2. a
3. b
4. c
5. d
6. d
7. b

GRM BIBLE SCHOOL

Reconnecting With Israel

Unit 2

GRM BIBLE SCHOOL

RECONNECTING WITH ISRAEL

UNIT 2

PART 1

Lesson 7 – Praying for the Salvation of Israel

1. "Salvation has come to the Gentiles to make them (the Jews) _____."
   a. Content
   b. Jealous
   c. Uncomfortable
   d. Wonder

2. "For if their rejection is the reconciliation of the world, what will their acceptance be but life from the _____?" (Romans 11:11-13)
   a. Dead
   b. Word
   c. Spirit
   d. Father

3. The Council of Nicaea began the development of anti-Semitism with the outcome of _____
   a. Dark Ages
   b. Nazi Shoa
   c. Pogroms
   d. All of the above

4. A Roman messiah does not attract the Jews; it must be a _____ Messiah.
   a. Greek
   b. Loving
   c. Jewish
   d. Powerful

5. True or False: Kabalah is witchcraft.
   a. True
   b. False

6. Since the time after the Council of Nicaea the Church has been _____ their original

Jewish roots.

    a. Divorced from

    b. Celebrating

    c. Embracing

    d. United with

7. Promises from Ezekiel 36:24-28 include
    a. For I will take you out of the nations & bring you back into your own land.
    b. I will sprinkle clean water on you and you will be clean.
    c. I will put my spirit in you.
    d. All of the above

ANSWERS

1. b
2. a
3. d
4. c
5. a
6. a
7. d

GRM BIBLE SCHOOL

RECONNECTING WITH ISRAEL

UNIT 2

PART 2

Lesson 8 – Praying for the Salvation of Israel

1. All of Ezekiel 36 is the "I Wills" of God concerning the restoration of _____.
   a. The Church
   b. Sinners
   c. The Nations
   d. Israel

2. True or False: Jews do not need to convert to Christianity. Jews need to accept Yeshua as their Messiah and get saved.
   a. True
   b. False

3. Yeshua is the real Hebrew birth name of Jesus, which the angel Gabriel gave Joseph to call Him. Yeshua means "_____".
   a. Son of God
   b. Salvation
   c. Prince of Peace
   d. Our Righteousness

4. We should pray, according to Ezekiel 36:24-26, for Israel to
   a. Receive a new heart and a new spirit
   b. Be sprinkled with clean water, to cleanse them from all their idols
   c. Return back to their land
   d. All of the above

5. Key to redemption of all _____ is their coming back to the Land (making Aliyah).
   a. Christians
   b. Believers
   c. Israel
   d. Catholics

6. When we say 'Yes' to Yeshua, we are given a new heart and a new spirit. God begins to _____ His

Word in our hearts.
- a. Write
- b. Reject
- c. Erase
- d. Change

7. It is important to pray because Yeshua will not come back until _____ say, "Blessed is He who comes in the Name of the Lord."
   - a. Christians
   - b. Muslims
   - c. Israelis
   - d. The Gentiles

ANSWERS

1. d
2. a
3. b
4. d
5. c
6. a
7. c

GRM BIBLE SCHOOL

Key of Abraham, Israel Our Mother

Unit 3

GRM BIBLE SCHOOL

KEY OF ABRAHAM

UNIT 3

PART 1

Lesson 9 – Israel Our Mother

1. The Key of Abraham (based on Genesis 12:3) outlines the promises given to Abraham regarding _____ and _____ , depending upon how he and his seed is treated by the nations of the earth.
   a. Prosperity and destiny
   b. Blessing and cursing
   c. Death and destruction
   d. Heaven and Hell

2. Genesis 22:17-18 states, "In your _____ all the nations of the earth will be blessed.
   a. Seed (offspring)
   b. Name
   c. Word
   d. None of the above

3. Exodus 20:12 is the first commandment with a _____ : "Honor your father and your mother so that your days may be long (a lengthy and prosperous life) in the Land that the Lord your God gives you".
   a. Promise
   b. Warning
   c. Curse
   d. All of the above

4. Israel is the _____ of the Church.
   a. Leader
   b. Head
   c. Mother
   d. Father

5. God takes very seriously the command not to curse (Qlala – "take lightly, dishonor, disrespect") your _____ and elders.
   a. Teachers
   b. Parents

c. Government

   d. Siblings

6. Israel has been a _____ to the nations by bringing the entire Holy Scriptures and Yeshua the Messiah.

   a. Curse

   b. Hindrance

   c. Blessing

   d. Problem

7. A common dominator of youth in mental hospitals is their hatred towards _____.

   a. Siblings

   b. Parents

   c. Finances

   d. Teachers

ANSWERS

1. b
2. a
3. a
4. c
5. b
6. c
7. b

GRM BIBLE SCHOOL

KEY OF ABRAHAM

UNIT 3

PART 2

Lesson 10 – Israel Our Mother

1. Israel is not the Church today; The Church (gentile Christians) is called to be _____ Israel, the Olive Tree.
   a. Grafted into
   b. Protector of
   c. Against
   d. Independent of

2. True or False: God has chosen Israel to be a Mother to the nations.
   a. True
   b. False

3. "My people are destroyed for lack of knowledge. Since you have forgotten the law (Torah) of your God I will also _____ your children." Hosea 4:6
   a. Visit
   b. Destroy
   c. Forget
   d. Remember

4. Anyone who disrespects or dishonors Israel will eventually come under the _____ of God.
   a. Judgment
   b. Blessing
   c. Grace
   d. All of the above

5. Israel was called to teach the nations the righteous standards of the Living God. "For I give you sound teaching, do not _____ my instruction." Proverbs 4:1, 2
   a. Change
   b. Abandon
   c. Compromise
   d. Embrace

6. Formation of the State of Israel in 1948 is a testimony that God is faithful to His _____.
   a. Word
   b. Covenant
   c. Promises
   d. All of the above

7. End-time Revival is about restoration between parents and their children, restoration between children and their parents, and restoration between the Church and _____.
   a. Holy Scriptures
   b. State
   c. Israel
   d. Holy giving

ANSWERS

1. a
2. a
3. c
4. a
5. b
6. d
7. c

GRM BIBLE SCHOOL

Revival of Reconciliation

Unit 4

GRM BIBLE SCHOOL

REVIVAL OF RECONCILIATION

UNIT 4

PART 1

Lesson 11

1. The Key of Abraham is based on Genesis 12: ____.
   a. 1
   b. 3
   c. 5
   d. 7

2. The Ten Commandments can be called the "Heavenly _____."
   a. Mandate
   b. Map
   c. Road map
   d. Constitution

3. When relationships between children and parents are strained it causes the land to be _____.
   a. Fertile
   b. Unbalanced
   c. Cursed
   d. None of the above

4. True or False: Restoration between the children and the parents is the key to End Times Revival.
   a. True
   b. False

5. The Spirit of _____ comes to restore.
   a. Wisdom
   b. Forgiveness
   c. David
   d. Elijah

6. Malachi 4:4 tells us how important it is to remember the _____ of Moses.
   a. Mistakes

b. Family
   c. Instruction (Torah)
   d. Days

7. In this End of times, God is restoring the hearts of the fathers to the sons - the Jewish people to their _____.
   a. Tribes
   b. Traditions
   c. Messiah
   d. All of the above

ANSWERS

1. b
2. d
3. c
4. a
5. d
6. c
7. c

GRM BIBLE SCHOOL

REVIVAL OF RECONCILIATION

UNIT 4

PART 2

Lesson 12

1. True or False: The Gospel is brought from Zion to the nations through the Jewish Messiah.
    a. True
    b. False

2. A key factor for coming under either the wrath or favor of the Lord is "Those that _____ My name." (Malachi 4)
    a. Fear
    b. Blaspheme
    c. Curse
    d. Honor

3. Malachi 4:2; "The sun of righteousness will rise with healing in its _____."
    a. Mouth
    b. Hand
    c. Wings
    d. None of the above

4. The _____ of the garment is where the tassels are placed (Num. 15:37-40) – reminding us of His commandments & the blessing of covenant relationship with the Father through faith.
    a. Sleeve
    b. Top
    c. Front
    d. Corner

5. Matthew 9:20-22 speaks of a woman with an issue of blood. She "touched the tassel of His cloak" and was made whole, as there is _____ in His (Messiah's) garment.
    a. Shalom
    b. Healing
    c. Comfort
    d. Unity

6. God is calling us to open our hearts so His Torah (_____ in Righteousness) will be written inside by the Holy Spirit.
    a. Suggestions
    b. Instructions
    c. Deeds
    d. Traditions

7. Christians who know Yeshua as a _____ will make the Jews jealous.
    a. Jew
    b. Priest
    c. Lion
    d. Man

ANSWERS

1. a
2. a
3. c
4. d
5. b
6. b
7. a

GRM BIBLE SCHOOL

REVIVAL OF RECONCILIATION

UNIT 4

PART 3

Lesson 13

1. The plan of God from the beginning is that Israel would be like a mother to the nations, bringing the_____ to the nations.
    a. Word of God
    b. Laws and Commandments
    c. Prophetic Writings
    d. All of the above

2. When we reject any portion of scripture, we are rejecting the Word _____. (ref. John 1:1 - "In the beginning was the Word and the Word was God." and John 1:14 - "The Word became flesh and dwelt among us.")
    a. Covenant
    b. Himself
    c. Validity
    d. Itself

3. Jeremiah 31:31 states, "Behold, days are coming," declares the Lord, "when I will make a new (renewed) _____ with the house of Israel and with the house of Judah."
    a. Treaty
    b. Agreement
    c. Covenant
    d. Law

4. The only sign that we are in the New Covenant is that we have the Torah, the Laws and Commandments of God, written in our _____.
    a. Mind
    b. Heart
    c. Bible
    d. Soul

5. In the New Covenant, the Laws and Commandments are not obsolete, they have just changed _____.
    a. Meanings

- b. Nationalities
- c. Locations
- d. Applications

6. Yeshua said, "Do not think that I came to abolish the Law or the Prophets". Saying that the Law is done away with is _____ doctrine
   - a. Legal
   - b. True
   - c. Correct
   - d. False

7. The commandments of God convict us of sin and cause us to _____ and walk in the ways of God. (Romans 7:7) - Subjecting ourselves to the Law of God is walking in the light.
   - a. Repent
   - b. Stumble
   - c. Rebel
   - d. Harden

ANSWERS

1. d
2. b
3. c
4. b
5. c
6. d
7. a

GRM BIBLE SCHOOL

REVIVAL OF RECONCILIATION

UNIT 4

PART 4

Lesson 14

1. True or False: "Honor your father and your mother," (Exodus 20:1) is not conditional - we should honor our parents even when they are imperfect.

    a. True

    b. False

2. _____ means "instructions in righteousness."

    a. Doctrine

    b. Commandments

    c. Scripture

    d. Torah

3. "The Law is _____" (Psalm 19:8) and "The commandment is holy and righteous and good." (Romans 7:12)

    a. For Jews

    b. Obsolete

    c. Perfect

    d. Burdensome

4. Matthew 5:17; "Do not think I have come to _____ the Law or the Prophets."

    a. Teach

    b. Follow

    c. Abolish

    d. Honor

5. Shabbat Shalom is a greeting. Shabbat means "to go on strike, to cease _____." Shalom means "Peace, well-being, wholeness, and prosperity".

    a. Eating

    b. Entertainment

    c. Functioning

    d. Working

6. End-times Revival is about _____: that of our God - the relationship of Israel to the nations – and also the father in your own family.
    a. Fatherhood
    b. People
    c. Souls
    d. Nations

7. God wants us to accept the fatherhood of God: "We received the spirit of _____ as sons by which we cry out, "Abba Father!"
    a. Jacob
    b. Adoption
    c. Elijah
    d. Rebellion

ANSWERS

1. a
2. d
3. c
4. c
5. d
6. a
7. b

GRM BIBLE SCHOOL

REVIVAL OF RECONCILIATION

UNIT 4

PART 5

Lesson 15

1. "I am going to send you _____ the prophet. He will turn the hearts of the fathers to their children and the hearts of the children to their fathers." (Mal. 4:4, 5)
   a. Ezekiel
   b. Jeremiah
   c. Elijah
   d. Elisha

2. According to Romans 8:7-8 - When we do not subject ourselves to the law of _____, we cannot please Him.
   a. Yah / God
   b. Liberty
   c. Spirit of Life
   d. Grace

3. When we do not accept the fatherhood of our parents, we are called _____.
   a. Orphans
   b. Fools
   c. Independent
   d. Disciples

4. The _____ fear of God is when we run to the arms of God when we've sinned.
   a. Awful
   b. Holy
   c. Dread
   d. Teshuvah

5. "For all who are being led by the Spirit of God, these are _____ of God." (Romans 8:14)
   a. Messengers
   b. Enemies
   c. Angels

d. Sons

6. True or False - Restoration of Israel and the nations, restoring that strained relationship, is the Key to revival.
   a. True
   b. False

7. When we do not obey God's commandments, we possess a spirit of _____ and not adoption.
   a. Grace
   b. Orphan
   c. Salvation
   d. Supplication

ANSWERS

1. c
2. a
3. a
4. b
5. d
6. a
7. b

GRM BIBLE SCHOOL

Key of Abraham Revealed

Unit 5

GRM BIBLE SCHOOL

KEY OF ABRAHAM REVEALED

UNIT 5

PART 1

Lesson 16

1. By being kind (a blessing) to a Jewish woman named Naomi, a widow named Ruth changed _____.
   a. Locations
   b. Nationalities
   c. History
   d. Regions

2. Naomi tells her daughters-in-law to go back to _____ and their people.
   a. Bethlehem
   b. Moab
   c. Mahlon
   d. Perez

3. While gleaning in the harvested field Ruth meets _____, the owner of the field.
   a. Moab
   b. Orpah
   c. Boaz
   d. Elimelech

4. Naomi requested to be called Mara, which means _____.
   a. Bitter
   b. Poor
   c. Widow
   d. Peace

5. Ruth is one of only three _____ mentioned in the lineage of Yeshua.
   a. Gentiles
   b. Moabites
   c. Widows
   d. Women

6. According to Ruth 2:8-12 we read how Ruth put the _____ of Abraham in the lock - because she had blessed the family of Boaz, Boaz blessed her. (This is directly connected to Genesis 12:3).
   a. Principles
   b. Law
   c. Family
   d. Key

7. Ruth becomes one of the great grandmothers of _____.
   a. King David
   b. Jacob
   c. Yeshua
   d. Jesse

ANSWERS

1. c
2. b
3. c
4. a
5. d
6. d
7. a

GRM BIBLE SCHOOL

KEY OF ABRAHAM REVEALED

UNIT 5

PART 2

Lesson 17

1. Cornelius, a Roman centurion, was the first Gentile to be _____.
   a. Stoned
   b. Saved (born again)
   c. Persecuted
   d. Crucified

2. Cornelius was a man who feared God and gave _____ to the Jewish people. He knew how to apply the principles of Genesis 12:3, which is the Key of Abraham.
   a. His daughter
   b. Soldiers
   c. Alms (finances)
   d. Camels

3. In Acts 10:10-20 we read of Peter's vision where he saw clean and unclean animals, but the interpretation given by God was clearly not about animals - it is about unclean _____.
   a. Practices
   b. Hygiene
   c. Worship
   d. People

4. True or False: It is impossible for Gentiles to receive the power of the Holy Spirit because they are unclean.
   a. True
   b. False

5. Peter tells the _____ about Yeshua the Messiah (Acts 10:38-48) and the Holy Spirit fell upon all those who were listening to the message. All the circumcised believers who came with Peter were amazed, because the gift of the Holy Spirit had also been poured out on the Gentiles.
   a. Gospel
   b. Lies
   c. Reasoning
   d. Deception

6. Revival is the Key of _____ at its best – the first key used for revival and salvation to come to the Gentiles, which will also be used at the End of Times.
   a. David
   b. Salvation
   c. Abraham
   d. Moses

7. The message had to come from a Jew (Peter, in this case) because "_____ is of the Jews" (John 4:22)
   a. Prophecy
   b. Salvation
   c. Prosperity
   d. Religion

ANSWERS

1. b
2. c
3. d
4. b
5. a
6. c
7. b

GRM BIBLE SCHOOL

KEY OF ABRAHAM REVEALED

UNIT 5

PART 3

Lesson 18

1. After 40 years of wandering, the Israelites are ready to possess the Promised Land and send 2 spies to Jericho. They meet a prostitute named _____.
   a. Hannah
   b. Esther
   c. Rahab
   d. Rebekah

2. This prostitute hid the spies and, because of her kind act, she and her household were spared from the complete destruction of Jericho. She is even listed in the genealogy of _____, showing the Key of Abraham (Gen. 12:3) in operation once again.
   a. Yeshua
   b. Abraham
   c. David
   d. Moses

3. The Scarlet Cord represented the _____ of the Lamb and the Covenant that God has with Israel, declaring into the spiritual realm that this home was protected. (Joshua 2:18, 19)
   a. Religion
   b. Blood
   c. Reality
   d. Image

4. True or False: God honors those who honor Israel.
   a. True
   b. False

5. The New Covenant was not made with the _____; it was made with the Jews.
   a. Romans
   b. Pharisees
   c. Sadducees
   d. Gentiles

6. God is a God of _____. When we speak about the Key of Abraham, we speak about a _____ matter.
   a. Religion
   b. Faith
   c. Covenant
   d. Worship

7. Joshua 6:25 - "Rahab the harlot and her father's household and all she had, Joshua _____; and she has lived in the midst of Israel to this day, for she hid the messengers whom Joshua sent to spy out Jericho."
   a. Saved
   b. Cursed
   c. Dishonored
   d. Rebuked

ANSWERS

1. c
2. a
3. b
4. a
5. d
6. c
7. a

GRM BIBLE SCHOOL

Replacement Theology Revealed

Unit 6

GRM BIBLE SCHOOL

REPLACEMENT THEOLOGY REVEALED

UNIT 6

PART 1

Lesson 19

1. The New Covenant is a "renewed" covenant that Elohim, (God) made with _____ and Judah.
   a. Moses
   b. Abraham
   c. Israel
   d. David

2. True or False: Abraham is the father of every Gentile believer who believes in the Jewish Messiah Yeshua.
   a. True
   b. False

3. Those who bless Israel and do good to her will enjoy the favor, the blessing, the prosperity, and the wholeness of the _____ of Israel. (Gen. 12:3 – the Key of Abraham)
   a. Land
   b. Religion
   c. God
   d. None of the above

4. "Whoever curses you (Hebr. Qlala) I will curse (Hebr. Meerah)", according to Gen. 12:3. Two words used for curse are qlala, which is to dishonor or take lightly, and meerah meaning complete _____
   a. Destruction
   b. Annihilation
   c. Devastation
   d. All of the above

5. _____ 28:1-14 is a list of God's blessings; verses 15-68 lists all the curses.
   a. Genesis
   b. Exodus
   c. Deuteronomy
   d. Leviticus

6. Every time a nation rose up to take lightly the people of Israel that nation was destroyed; every empire that rose up against the people of Israel is _____ today.

    a. Prospering

    b. Blessed

    c. Glorious

    d. Nonexistent

7. The 4th century Church divorced itself from its Jewish roots through the _____ of Nicaea, which called for total separation between Christian Gentiles and the Jews / everything Jewish.

    a. Council

    b. Decree

    c. Declaration

    d. Liturgy

ANSWERS

1. c

2. a

3. c

4. d

5. c

6. d

7. a

GRM BIBLE SCHOOL

REPLACEMENT THEOLOGY REVEALED

UNIT 6

PART 2

Lesson 20

1. The natural descendants of _____ are the people of Israel and today are called the Jewish people.
   a. Moses
   b. Abraham
   c. Yeshua
   d. Paul

2. In the year 325 C.E., Roman Emperor Constantine established the Council of Nicaea and adopted _____ as the religion of the Empire.
   a. Christianity
   b. Judaism
   c. Islam
   d. Buddhism

3. The Council of Nicaea (Replacement Theology) states that Jews killed Yeshua so they deserved to be killed. Therefore, it's Christian duty to _____ the Jewish people.
   a. Bless
   b. Persecute
   c. Assist
   d. Love

4. Until the 4th century Jews and Gentiles were _____. Because Gentiles were in the majority, Constantine decided the Jews weren't needed anymore
   a. Persecuted
   b. Ignored
   c. Divided
   d. Together

5. The Hebrew Holy Scriptures "_____ Testament" became obsolete.
   a. New
   b. Old

c. Holy

   d. Replacement

6. True or False: Under Constantine Israel is replaced by the Church.

   a. True

   b. False

7. Yeshua prayed for _____.

   a. Jews

   b. Gentiles

   c. Unity

   d. Israel

ANSWERS

1. b

2. a

3. b

4. d

5. b

6. a

7. c

GRM BIBLE SCHOOL

REPLACEMENT THEOLOGY REVEALED

UNIT 6

PART 3

Lesson 21

1. True or False: The Council of Nicaea brought division to the Church and brought the curse instead of the blessing, eventually producing the Dark Ages.
   a. True
   b. False

2. Because of the division, a Tower of Babel system began, creating a multitude of denominations; this is described in Genesis 11:4 - "Come, let us build ourselves a city, with a tower that reaches to the heavens, so that we may make a _____ for ourselves."
   a. Place
   b. Country
   c. Name
   d. People

3. Yeshua, the Hebrew name of Jesus, means _____.
   a. Beloved
   b. Joy
   c. Anointed
   d. Salvation

4. The Lord speaks about us as living stones (1st Peter 2:5). Bricks on the other hand represent false theologies, not based on the Word of God, which replace the original _____ foundation of faith.
   a. Hebrew
   b. Christian
   c. Abrahamic
   d. Adamic

5. Martin Luther tried to restore the original foundation, but stumbled in the area of the Jews. His book, On the Jews and Their Lies, outlined actions to be taken against Jewish people which included:
   a. All prayer books and Talmudic books be taken from them
   b. Set fire to synagogues and schools
   c. Safe conduct be abolished on highways for the Jews

d. All of the above

6. The fruit of Christianity after the Council of Nicaea included:
   a. Miracles ceased
   b. Anti-Semitism
   c. Birth of the Dark Ages
   d. All of the above

7. God is calling us back to the original foundations of faith, back to the faith of the _____ Apostles.
   a. Jewish
   b. First century
   c. A & B above
   d. Christian

ANSWERS

1. a
2. c
3. d
4. a
5. d
6. d
7. c

GRM BIBLE SCHOOL

REPLACEMENT THEOLOGY REVEALED

UNIT 6

PART 4

Lesson 22

1. True or False: The Key of Abraham opens and closes nations and people for blessing.
   a. True
   b. False

2. The Christianity established by Constantine in 325 C.E. called for a separation or divorce from the _____ foundations of the faith
   a. Hebrew
   b. Religious
   c. Pagan
   d. Unholy

3. Constantine's divorce from the original Jewish roots meant that Jews and Gentile Believers in Yeshua could not
   a. Keep Sabbath
   b. Celebrate the Feasts of God
   c. Keep the laws and commandments written in the Torah
   d. All of the above

4. The New Covenant is when the laws and commandments of God are _____ in our heart. (Jeremiah 31:31-34)
   a. Irrelevant
   b. Written
   c. Rejected
   d. No longer

5. True or False: Being saved by grace through faith means that the laws of God are done away with.
   a. True
   b. False

6. The job of the Jews is to be a light unto the nations through:
   a. Yeshua
   b. The Jewish Apostles and Prophets

c. Bringing the Word of Yahveh and salvation to the nations

   d. All of the above

7. Nazi Germany stated that Jews killed Christ and deserved to die; however, Yeshua was not _____ (according to John 10:17-18) but was willingly sacrificed.

   a. Murdered

   b. Crucified

   c. Spit upon

   d. Flogged

ANSWERS

1. a

2. a

3. d

4. b

5. b

6. d

7. a

GRM BIBLE SCHOOL

REPLACEMENT THEOLOGY REVEALED

UNIT 6

PART 5

LESSON 23

1. True or False: Replacement Theology quenches the Holy Spirit and does not allow the Key of Abraham to go into the lock and open the revival of nations.

    a. True

    b. False

2. Prior to Council of Nicaea the first century Church was well connected to its roots, grafted into the Olive Tree of _____.

    a. David

    b. Judah

    c. Israel

    d. Abraham

3. The first century Church only had the "Old Testament:" Books of the Law - Five books of _____ (Torah), the Prophets, and the Writings (like Proverbs and Psalms).

    a. Moses

    b. Commandments

    c. Joshua

    d. None of the Above

4. One of the early Church Fathers was Eusebius (263-339 C.E.) who stated, "Promises of the Hebrew Scriptures were for _____ and not the Jews." & "The curses were for the Jews."

    a. Everyone

    b. Romans

    c. Greeks

    d. Christians

5. Constantine outlawed keeping Shabbat and established Sunday will be the holy day _____ Shabbat.

    a. Memorializing

    b. Replacing

    c. Celebrating

    d. None of the above

6. Easter is named after the goddess Ishtar, who was the goddess of _____.
    a. War
    b. The sun
    c. The moon
    d. Fertility

7. Celebrating the resurrection of Yeshua is good, but not with "other gods" (or goddesses) and not with _____ rites.
    a. Pagan
    b. Unholy
    c. A & B above
    d. Musical

ANSWERS

1. a
2. c
3. a
4. d
5. b
6. d
7. c

GRM BIBLE SCHOOL

REPLACEMENT THEOLOGY REVEALED

UNIT 6

PART 6

LESSON 24

1. The issue of Replacement Theology is an awakening issue; God is calling us to wake up and come out of those things that are _____.
   a. Holy
   b. Unholy
   c. Unifying
   d. Uplifting

2. The Council of Nicaea replaced:
   a. The holy seasons and the holy timings given by Yahveh.
   b. Feast names for pagan names/holidays.
   c. Shabbat with Sunday worship.
   d. All of the above

3. True or False: With the Holy Spirit we can keep all of God's commandments, not under a spirit of legalism, but under a spirit of holiness and righteousness.
   a. True
   b. False

4. Easter (The Feast of _____) includes sexual worship which produces babies nine months later. These babies were slaughtered at 3 months old as an offering to the goddess (on her annual Feast day); eggs were dipped into their blood and displayed, so people could see how many had been slaughtered.
   a. Ishtar
   b. Passover
   c. Unleavened Bread
   d. Pentecost

5. Easter and Passover: Constantine established Easter, which replaced Passover. Yeshua was crucified on _____ and rose from the dead on the Feast of First Fruits (1st Corinthians 15:20 - "But now Christ has been raised from the dead, the first fruits of those who are asleep.")
   a. Sabbath
   b. Easter
   c. Passover

d. Sunday

6. Yeshua could not have been born on December 25th - this is the pagan _____ solstice celebration. Yeshua was born during the feast of Sukkot (Feast of Tabernacles).

   a. Spring
   b. Winter
   c. Holy
   d. All of the above

7. Christmas Trees and things that "look nice" do not mean they are holy and acceptable to God. We are called to be _____ - then our prayers will be answered. (Proverbs 28:9)

   a. Godly
   b. Obedient
   c. Religious
   d. A & B above

ANSWERS

1. b
2. d
3. a
4. a
5. c
6. b
7. d

GRM BIBLE SCHOOL

REPLACEMENT THEOLOGY REVEALED

UNIT 6

PART 7

Lesson 25

1. What's the big deal about preaching the Jewish roots to the Church? It's a matter of _____ and _____ - On the third day, if she's not replanted back, she shall surely die.
   a. Night and Day
   b. Life and Death
   c. Truth or Lies
   d. Black and White

2. God has NOT forgotten the Jewish people. Romans 11:11 states, "Salvation has come to the Gentiles, to make them (Jews) _____."
   a. Afraid
   b. Nervous
   c. Jealous
   d. Unite

3. Replacement Theology cannot make the Jewish people jealous because of:
   a. Pagan feasts and celebrations
   b. Anti-Semitism
   c. People who say they love God but hate Israel
   d. All of the above

4. Yeshua cannot come back until _____ say, "Baruch haba baShem Adonai" (Blessed is he who comes in the Name of the Lord).
   a. Muslims
   b. Jews
   c. Christians
   d. Pagans

5. Christians can become steppingstones by repentance and by restoring the _____ foundations of faith in the Messiah.
   a. Original Hebrew
   b. Roman

c. Greek

d. Babylonian

6. Israel must be restored – first to the land, then to the _____.
   a. People
   b. Torah
   c. Church
   d. Messiah

7. True or False: Yeshua wants to reveal Himself to the Jewish people as the Jewish Messiah.
   a. True
   b. False

ANSWERS

1. b
2. c
3. d
4. b
5. a
6. d
7. a

GRM BIBLE SCHOOL

The Fear and Silence of God

Unit 7

GRM BIBLE SCHOOL

THE FEAR AND SILENCE OF GOD

UNIT 7

PART 1

Lesson 26 – The Fear of the Lord

1. Jonah teaches us what the fear of God isn't - then he teaches us what the fear of God is. When fear takes us _____ the presence of the Lord, that is the wrong fear.
    a. Away from
    b. Closer to
    c. Towards
    d. Into

2. When Adam sinned, they ran away from the presence of the Lord and lost their _____ which was turned over to Satan.
    a. Mind
    b. Confidence
    c. Authority
    d. Children

3. Adam also hid from the presence of the Lord and escaped his calling; the calling of Adam was to _____.
    a. Create
    b. Work
    c. Take dominion
    d. Destroy

4. There is a bitter price to escape your _____.
    a. Responsibility
    b. Calling
    c. Identity
    d. Adoption

5. True or False: While God speaks there is no hope available.
    a. True
    b. False

6. God sent a prophet to provoke _____.
   a. Violence
   b. Jealousy
   c. Shame
   d. Repentance

7. What kind of fear of God throws you out of the presence of God? The _____ one.
   a. Wrong
   b. Best
   c. Only
   d. All of the above

ANSWERS

1. a
2. c
3. c
4. b
5. b
6. d
7. a

GRM BIBLE SCHOOL

THE FEAR AND SILENCE OF GOD

UNIT 7

PART 2

Lesson 27 – The Fear of the Lord

1. Jonah teaches us about the fear of the _____.
   a. Devil
   b. King
   c. People
   d. Lord

2. Matthew 16:25 gives a warning to not be like Jonah, who tried to preserve his _____.
   a. Family
   b. Life
   c. Money
   d. Reputation

3. Judgment must first begin with the House of _____. (1st Peter 4:17)
   a. Pharoah
   b. Abraham
   c. God
   d. David

4. True or False: When God doesn't speak anymore is a point of no return.
   a. True
   b. False

5. When we repent, we get the _____ of God back.
   a. Sense
   b. Presence
   c. People
   d. Land

6. Regarding repentance: You are sad, not because of condemnation, but because you broke the heart of the _____.
   a. Father

b. King
   c. Ruler
   d. Prophet

7. God is calling us in this End of times to rise up like _____.
   a. Bethlehem
   b. Jerusalem
   c. Ninevah
   d. Babylon

ANSWERS

1. d
2. b
3. c
4. a
5. b
6. a
7. c

GRM BIBLE SCHOOL

THE FEAR AND SILENCE OF GOD

UNIT 7

PART 3

Lesson 28 – The Silence of God

1. While God is restoring _____ there is judgment across the nations that have come against Israel. (Zechariah 2:7-13)
   a. Faith
   b. Israel
   c. Finances
   d. Nations

2. The promise and judgment happen at the same time; God gave the promise to Abraham at the same time He is about to judge _____ and Gomorrah. (Genesis 18:10-21)
   a. Israel
   b. Judah
   c. Sodom
   d. None of the above

3. True or False: As long as God is still speaking God is extending mercy. The moment He becomes silent there will be no more time for repentance.
   a. True
   b. False

4. God loves everyone, but He hates their _____.
   a. Sacrifices
   b. Faith
   c. Godliness
   d. Sin

5. America needs to go into _____.
   a. Retreat
   b. Hiding
   c. Repentance
   d. Zion

6. Judgment and revival happen at the same time: On one hand God is saying to the faithful, "I am going to revive you." On the other hand, for the ones who are _____, He is saying judgment.
   a. Unrepentant
   b. Merciful
   c. Seeking Him
   d. All of the above

7. Even though Israel needs to repent, God is still going to _____ the nations that come against Israel.
   a. Revive
   b. Judge
   c. Bless
   d. Favor

ANSWERS

1. b
2. c
3. a
4. d
5. c
6. a
7. b

GRM BIBLE SCHOOL

The Eternal Gospel

Unit 8

GRM BIBLE SCHOOL

THE ETERNAL GOSPEL

UNIT 8

PART 1

Lesson 29

1. The _____ Gospel means this is the gospel (truth, good news) forever.
    a. New Covenant
    b. Eternal
    c. Old Covenant
    d. None of the above

2. True or False: Fear of God is the foundation of the Eternal Gospel.
    a. True
    b. False

3. According to Isaiah 11:3, _____ will delight in the fear of the Lord.
    a. Everyone
    b. Believers
    c. No one
    d. Yeshua

4. Psalm 111:10 states, "The fear of the Lord is the beginning of _____."
    a. Wisdom
    b. Health
    c. Joy
    d. Peace

5. Humility is a key for _____, as stated in 2 Chron. 7:14.
    a. Revival
    b. Believers (My people)
    c. Healing
    d. All of the above

6. Acts 5:1-11 tells about the deceit of Ananias and Sapphira, who were exposed by a _____ of Knowledge through Peter; their judgment brought great fear to the Church.
    a. Fear

b. Word

   c. Book

   d. Lack

7. Without the fear of _____ there is no revival.

   a. Death

   b. Man

   c. Punishment

   d. God

ANSWERS

1. b

2. a

3. d

4. a

5. d

6. b

7. d

GRM BIBLE SCHOOL

THE ETERNAL GOSPEL

UNIT 8
PART 2

LESSON 30

1. The Eternal Gospel starts with the words, "_____." (Rev. 14:6-8)
   a. Humble yourself
   b. Fear God
   c. Woe to you sinners
   d. Worship Him

2. Fear of God was prevalent in the early _____ in Jerusalem 2,000 years ago.
   a. Church
   b. Days
   c. Pagans
   d. All of the above

3. The early Church had the glory because:
   a. The people were filled with the power of the Holy Spirit
   b. People obeyed God's commandments
   c. The people were full of His Word
   d. All of the above

4. Haggai 2:9 states, "The latter glory of this house will be _____ the former."
   a. The same as
   b. Less than
   c. Greater than
   d. None of the above

5. True or False: If the Eternal Gospel is not preached there will be no glory.
   a. True
   b. False

6. It was very clear to the 12 Apostles that God had not done away with His _____.
   a. Disciples
   b. Commandments

c. People

   d. Messiah

7. The original Hebrew foundation was replaced with a mixture of _____ in the Church and a Babylonian foundation.

   a. Races

   b. Languages

   c. Denominations

   d. Paganism

ANSWERS

1. b
2. a
3. d
4. c
5. a
6. b
7. d

GRM BIBLE SCHOOL

THE ETERNAL GOSPEL

UNIT 8

PART 3

Lesson 31

1. Revelation 14:6-8 states, "And I saw another angel flying in midheaven, having an _____ to preach to those who live on the earth, and to every nation and tribe and tongue and people."
    a. Evangelist
    b. Eternal gospel
    c. Apostle
    d. Edict

2. While God is _____ the Eternal Gospel, Babylon the Great is falling.
    a. Restoring
    b. Ending
    c. Condemning
    d. Concealing

3. True or False: Babylon represents every pagan religious system.
    a. True
    b. False

4. Before Yeshua can return the original Hebrew _____ of the Church need to be restored and Israel needs to be restored.
    a. Style
    b. Language
    c. Foundations
    d. Letters

5. Proverbs 1:7 states, "The _____ of the LORD is the beginning of knowledge; Fools despise wisdom and instruction."
    a. Word
    b. Name
    c. Ways
    d. Fear

6. "Fear God, and give Him glory, because the hour of His _____ has come." (Revelation 14:7)
   a. Salvation
   b. Judgment
   c. Sanctification
   d. Cleansing

7. In Revelation 21 we read that the foundation stones of the New Jerusalem are _____ (names of the 12 Apostles) and the gates are Israelite (names of the 12 Tribes).
   a. Greek
   b. Christian
   c. Catholic
   d. Jewish

ANSWERS

1. b
2. a
3. a
4. c
5. d
6. b
7. d

GRM BIBLE SCHOOL

THE ETERNAL GOSPEL

UNIT 8
PART 4

LESSON 32

1. The Eternal Gospel produces the fear of God, which brings with it _____ and righteousness.
   a. Peace
   b. Joy
   c. Holiness
   d. Love

2. The Eternal Gospel is restoration of _____ and is a key to revival.
   a. Peace
   b. Knowledge
   c. Love
   d. Unity

3. The beginning of the Gospel is the preaching of John the Baptizer, who spoke about _____.
   a. Repentance
   b. Faith
   c. Tithing
   d. Adultery

4. In John 14:15 Yeshua states, "If you _____ Me, you will keep My commandments."
   a. Love
   b. Honor
   c. Hate
   d. Believe

5. God must _____ sin; therefore, we must walk in the fear of God and repent of our sins, not continue walking in them under the guise of being a Christian.
   a. Allow
   b. Embrace
   c. Judge
   d. Tolerate

6. True or False: God wants His house transparent and pure crystal clear; therefore, in order to be the Bride that is pure and holy, God is calling us to obey the Gospel, not only believe it.
    a. True
    b. False

7. Solomon summed up the "whole duty of man" when he wrote in Ecclesiastes 12:13, "Fear God and _____."
    a. Then we celebrate
    b. Keep His commandments
    c. Live in peace
    d. Take dominion

ANSWERS

1. c
2. d
3. a
4. a
5. c
6. a
7. b

GRM BIBLE SCHOOL

THE ETERNAL GOSPEL

UNIT 8

PART 5

Lesson 33

1. The Lord has to judge His house and _____ it, so we will be a pure and holy Bride, full of His glory.
    a. Change
    b. Cleanse
    c. Destroy
    d. Mark

2. True or False: The New Jerusalem is both a city and a people, full of the glory of God.
    a. True
    b. False

3. The entire New Jerusalem is of _____ essence.
    a. Hebrew
    b. Babylonian
    c. Christian
    d. None of the above

4. The Lion of the Tribe of Judah opens the Book of _____. (Rev. 5:5)
    a. Life
    b. Revelation
    c. Messiah
    d. Judgment

5. The Gospel of the Kingdom right now has been "watered down" and has not been pure, crystal clear water – the kind which provokes repentance, causing you to return to the arms of the _____.
    a. Priest
    b. Pastor
    c. Father
    d. Church

6. Any gospel that omits repentance or a call for purity, righteousness, and holiness is not the

_____ Gospel.
   a. Christian
   b. True
   c. Covenantial
   d. None of the above

7. _____ comes to restore purity, holiness, & righteousness in order to return the glory that Adam lost when he broke God's commandment; Adam stayed lost because he didn't repent, as unrighteous fear caused him to hide under his own excuses.
   a. Solomon
   b. Satan
   c. Yeshua
   d. Paul

ANSWERS

1. b
2. a
3. a
4. d
5. c
6. b
7. c

GRM BIBLE SCHOOL

FOUNDATIONS OF FAITH REVEALED

Reading Schedule

1. The Healing Power of the Roots
2. Grafted In
3. Sheep Nations
4. Vision Negev

BOOK 1

Healing Power of the Roots

1. Emperor Constantine, a sun worshipper, adopted _____ as the official religion of the Eastern Roman Empire in 325 AD (adopted at the Council of Nicea) totally divorcing itself from its Jewish/Biblical roots (including the law of Moses) and changed the Biblical seasons & feasts.
   a. Christianity
   b. Judaism
   c. Romanism
   d. None of the above

2. Preaching on the Jewish roots of our faith would be the key for true disciples: being connected to our roots is a matter of _____.
   a. Preference
   b. Life and Death
   c. Doctrines
   d. Denominations

3. Hearts that contain _____, whether in a hidden form or in a very obvious one, cannot receive God's revelation and God's healing.
   a. Lies
   b. Deception
   c. Anti-Semitism

d. Anger

4. Believers in the 4th Century compromised their beliefs in order to accept Constantine's "peace treaty" (a new faith mixed with pagan customs) because it came at a time of intense _____.
   a. Persecution
   b. Rioting
   c. Evangelizing
   d. Famine

5. In Matt. 7:23 Yeshua looked into their heart, stating that those who were working for God (seeing miracles occur and demons cast out) were not allowed into the Kingdom of Heaven because they were without _____.
   a. Spiritual maturity
   b. Law (Torah)
   c. Oil in their lamps
   d. Wedding clothes

6. Paul never encouraged anyone to break the Torah, but being divorced from our Jewish/Biblical roots causes us to:
   a. Defy the laws of the Lord
   b. Be ignorant of the law
   c. Misinterpret scripture
   d. All of the above

7. True or False: The identity of the Church (separated from its family roots and with a lack of belonging) has rejection as a root issue and root cause of most of the emotional problems of God's children.
   a. True
   b. False

8. Because of the "rejection of Ephraim" that came through Gentile bloodlines, the presence of _____ causes wounds of rejection to open and starts a reaction of anti-Semitism.
   a. A prophet
   b. The Jews
   c. The Holy Spirit
   d. Christians

9. Repentance and Humility are the keys against age-old destructive _____. (see Prov. 27:4 and Is. 11:12,13)
   a. Lies
   b. Doctrine
   c. Jealousy
   d. Leaders

10. When we allow the law to be written on our heart and reconnect to our Biblical roots, we become one with

Israel. We are Grafted In (Rom. 11:17), belonging to the commonwealth of Israel – not having _____ Israel, but rejoined Israel.

a. Replaced
b. Persecuted
c. Adopted
d. Rejected

ANSWERS

1. a   2. b   3. c   4. a   5. b   6. d   7. a   8. b   9. c   10. a

GRM BIBLE SCHOOL

Book 2

Grafted In

1. Being grafted into the Olive Tree does not mean to be grafted into another religious system, but rather into a nation called _____ and into the Biblical lifestyle that is fashioned by the manual which shaped that nation from the beginning – the Bible.
   a. Greece
   b. Babylon
   c. Italy
   d. Israel

2. In year 325 AD the act of `de-grafting` or uprooting the Church from the Olive Tree was formalized and from that moment _____ begins to rule the Body - all traces of Judaism are removed from the Church and from the Messiah Himself!
   a. Replacement Theology
   b. Hinduism
   c. Selfishness
   d. Buddhism

3. True or False: After the Council of Nicea, everything Jewish was outlawed (including the Hebrew Holy Scriptures, the Hebrew name of the Messiah, the Biblical Feasts, the Torah etc.).
   a. True
   b. False

4. Exodus 31:16-17 says that the _____ is a PERPETUAL COVENANT and a SIGN FOREVER.
   a. Land
   b. Christmas
   c. Shabbat
   d. Lamb

5. The way to change the world's condition, from sin and wickedness to the knowledge of the glory of Yahveh, will occur by_____.
   a. Praying an hour a day
   b. Worship YHVH for 2 hours a day
   c. Obeying the Great Commission
   d. None of the above

6. True or False: The Torah was not only given for the Jewish People to keep these marvelous instructions for themselves, but rather for them to share them with the entire world and thus bring the world into the ways of THE BLESSING.
   a. True
   b. False

7. The Feast of Sukkot will be celebrated during the Millennium and it will be _____ for the nations.
   a. Mandatory
   b. Voluntary
   c. Forbidden
   d. Closed

8. When the New Testament speaks about the Word it always means _____.
   The New Testament portion of the Bible was canonized 300 years later.
   a. The book of Enoch
   b. The Torah/5 books of Moses
   c. The book of Psalms
   d. The Tanakh/The Old Testament

9. The Zadok-like priesthood of today is Apostolic/Prophetic, and they are sent to the Church to lead a Move of Holiness that tolerates _____.
   a. All faiths
   b. Idolatry
   c. No mixture
   d. Laziness

10. When the Ecclesia is restored to the Jewish Roots of her faith, then the Glory that will be within her, the Greatness of YAH restored in her, will cause Israel to see _____ and for many nations to turn to YAH and become Sheep Nations.
    a. Moses
    b. Messiah
    c. Elijah the Prophet
    d. Virgin Mary

ANSWERS

1. d   2. a   3. a   4. c   5. c   6. a   7. a   8. d   9. c   10. b

GRM BIBLE SCHOOL

Book 3

Sheep Nations

1. Israel is the centerpiece for the _____ of the Nations.
   a. Destruction
   b. Redemption
   c. End
   d. Armies

2. The Nations will be judged (as Sheep or Goat Nations) by 2 standards: first, by My Eternal, Unchanging Righteous _____ and, second, by how the Nations treat my Jewish people.
   a. Law
   b. Spirit
   c. Church
   d. Hand

3. There is no better spiritual strategy concerning each Nation than to lead that nation or ethnic group into _____ for sins of omission (what was not done to help) or sins of commission (what was done to do harm) against the Jews and the Nation of Israel.
   a. Fasting
   b. Mourning
   c. Rejoicing
   d. Repentance

4. True or False: Archbishop Bierman believes that in these end times the outpouring of Yah's glory will be on entire Nations, as He is calling a holy people unto Himself.
   a. True
   b. False

5. 1 Peter 4:17 states that the first to be judged is _____.
   a. America
   b. The Church (house of Yah)
   c. Christian Nations
   d. Israel

6. Today the Lord is calling the True Church to arise, calling Christians to:
   a. Get rid of pagan feasts and ungodly practices

    b. Get rid of watered-down gospels

    c. Go back to the same Torah Apostle Paul honored

    d. All of the above

7. Any Nation that will set the Torah of Yahveh as their righteous Constitutional Standard will be _____ and will become great.

    a. Judged

    b. Brought low

    c. Set on high

    d. All of the above

8. Abraham was chosen (to bring blessing to the Nations) because Yah knew he would embrace His commandments and teach his _____ after him. (Gen. 18:18, 19)

    a. Children

    b. Servants

    c. Enemies

    d. None of the above

9. As you follow The Ruth Way and turn the Key of _____ into the blessing position, your life will begin to shift.

    a. David

    b. Abraham

    c. Yeshua

    d. Boaz

10. Israel is Yah's firstborn, carrying the blessing of authority and double portion; Israel is the _____ Sheep Nation.

    a. Best

    b. Only

    c. Chief

    d. Favorite

ANSWERS

1. b   2. a   3. d   4. a   5. b   6. d   7. c   8. a   9. b   10. c

GRM BIBLE SCHOOL

BOOK 4

VISION NEGEV

1. True or False: 55% of the land allotted to modern day Israel is known as the Negev, the southern desert of Israel, starting south of Ashkelon (North Gate of Negev) and ending in Eilat on the Red Sea (South Gate of the Negev).
   a. True
   b. False

2. According to Yahveh, My Sephardic "lost" sheep are the Spanish Jews needing their _____ restored.
   a. Land
   b. Money
   c. Hope
   d. Identity

3. The Church of Santa Maria La Blanca was the Major _____ of Toledo, prior to the 1492 expulsion of Jews from Spain.
   a. Church
   b. Synagogue
   c. Center
   d. None of the above

4. Those who have forsaken their identity as Jews to appease authorities in the Spanish Inquisition are known as:
   a. Conversos
   b. Marranos
   c. Crypto Jews
   d. All of the above

5. Approx. 60 million descendants of lost Jews are being called back home to Israel, as described in Ezek. 36:24-25, and YHVH promises to cleanse them from all impurities and from all _____.
   a. Diseases
   b. Disunity
   c. Idols
   d. Lust

6. Prime Minister _____ saw that the future of Israel is depending on the settling of the Negev (Is.

35:1 CJB)

- a. Benjamin Netanyahu
- b. Golda Meir
- c. Menachem Begin
- d. David Ben Gurion

7. The miracle at Kibbutz Revivim, involving the blooming of _____ flowers, determined the future of Israel possessing the Negev.
    - a. Gladiola
    - b. Lavender
    - c. Tulip
    - d. Daisy

8. Eilat is a strategic place at the Southern Gate of the Negev overlooking the Mountains of _____ (Esau) – the spirit of Esau is none other than the spirit of Amalek (grandson of Esau – Gen. 26:12) and we know the memory of Amalek will be blotted out. Ref. Deut. 25:17-19
    - a. Egypt
    - b. Edom
    - c. Saudi Arabia
    - d. Jordan

9. As we see in Exod. 14:27-28, the city of Eilat on the _____ is the Gate of Defeat for all the enemies of Israel.
    - a. Galilee
    - b. Jordan River
    - c. Red Sea
    - d. Dead Sea

10. The Abrahamic Land Covenant is in effect and will be in effect to a _____ generations (Ps. 105:8-11, which also states that it is "forever"); therefore, Palestinians remaining in the land must surrender to the God of Israel, not Allah.
    - a. Thousand
    - b. Million
    - c. Hundred
    - d. None of the above

ANSWERS

1. a   2. d   3. b   4. d   5. c   6. d   7. a   8. b   9. c   10. a

GRM BIBLE SCHOOL

FOUNDATIONS OF FAITH REVEALED

Term Paper

INSTRUCTIONS

In four pages to ten pages, discuss what you have learned through Lessons 1-33 and the four books by Archbishop Dominiquae Bierman. Make sure to include the following points:

1. Trace the Jewish roots of the faith from the beginning with Abraham, through the Council of Nicaea, to modern times.

2. What are some of the things leading up to the council of Nicaea and the divorce from the Hebrew roots?

3. What is the fruit of the Council of Nicaea from the 4th century to the present day?

4. Explain the Key of Abraham and give some examples both in blessing and in curse. Include 20th century examples.

5. How does this relate to the fear of the Lord?

6. Discuss how all of this tie in with the Eternal Gospel.

Make sure to cite all references. Biblical references need book, chapter, and verse. For example: Isaiah 53:4-6. Book references for Archbishop's books need title and page number. Use quotation marks for direct quotes. Other material cite appropriately.

FORMAT

- Double spaced with 12pt font
- Your Name
- Title as, "Foundations of Faith Revealed Term Paper"
- Summary: This is a one paragraph summary of your term paper.
- Main Section: Make sure it has a logical flow with an introduction, main body, and conclusion.
- Practical Application: This is a separate section at the end. Include what have you learned and how you can use this information or how it can be applied in these end times. Include any new insights you may have.

GRM ISRAELI BIBLE SCHOOL
LEVEL 2: DISCOVERING THE HEBREW SCRIPTURES

STUDENT WORKBOOK
UNITS 9-12

www.grmbibleschool.com

info@grmbibleschool.com

GRM BIBLE SCHOOL

Israel Rediscovered

Unit 9

GRM BIBLE SCHOOL

REDISCOVERING GENESIS

UNIT 9

PART 1

Lesson 34

1. The Hebrew word "Beresheet" means:
   a. Genesis
   b. In the beginning
   c. The principal thing
   d. All of the above

2. Genesis 1:2 and on talks about everything connected with the _____
   a. Earth
   b. Heavens
   c. Both the Heavens and the earth
   d. None of the above

3. The Hebrew meaning of "Let there be light" is actually _____.
   a. And light came to be
   b. Light be
   c. There was light
   d. There was no light

4. The Word is _____.
   a. Flesh
   b. Nothing
   c. Yeshua
   d. None of the above

5. The Heroes of creation are _____.
   a. Elohim, The Word, Abraham
   b. Elohim, Ruach, Adam
   c. The Word, Ruach, Adam
   d. Elohim, Ruach, The Word

6. The Word and the Spirit work _____.
   a. Separately
   b. As one
   c. In two different places
   d. Independently

7. There is a _____ between Genesis 1:1 and Genesis 1:2.
   a. Separation
   b. Chaos
   c. Order
   d. Pause

ANSWERS

1. d
2. a
3. b
4. c
5. d
6. b
7. d

GRM BIBLE SCHOOL

REDISCOVERING GENESIS

UNIT 9

PART 2

Lesson 35

1. God is not a creator of chaos but of_____ and harmony.
    a. Beginning
    b. Earth
    c. Order
    d. Beauty

2. When this mighty archangel falls down to earth it causes _____.
    a. An explosion
    b. Calmness
    c. Chaos
    d. None of the above

3. The devil brings death, destruction, darkness, disorder: _____Vavohu.
    a. Tohu
    b. Order
    c. Disharmony
    d. All of the above

4. The "I wills" of Satan are trying to contend with the "I wills" of _____.
    a. Man
    b. Adam
    c. Snake
    d. God

5. Satan wants the throne of _____ on earth.
    a. God
    b. Adam
    c. Abraham
    d. None of the above

6. Satan wants to take the place of the Jewish people in the Holy _____.
   a. Mountain
   b. Place
   c. Jerusalem
   d. Temple

7. Satan wants to take the place of man because angels are not created in the _____ and likeness of Elohim.
   a. Picture
   b. Nature
   c. Order
   d. Image

ANSWERS

1. c
2. c
3. a
4. d
5. a
6. d
7. d

GRM BIBLE SCHOOL

REDISCOVERING GENESIS

UNIT 9

PART 3

Lesson 36

1. What happened to the earth was that Satan was thrown_____.
   a. Down
   b. Over
   c. Out
   d. None of the above

2. Luke 10:18 - "And He said to them, "I was watching Satan fall from _____ like lightning. "
   a. The sky
   b. Window
   c. Both A & B
   d. Heaven

3. The creator of wealth and the creator of worship is _____, the Creator of the Universe.
   a. Satan
   b. Adam
   c. The Almighty
   d. All of the above

4. The King of Babylon and the King of Tyre are another way of referring to _____.
   a. Man
   b. Lucifer
   c. Adam
   d. Yeshua

5. The Anti-Christ wants to sit on the _____ of Messiah.
   a. Mountain
   b. Altar
   c. Throne
   d. Both A and B

6. Bavel (or Babylon) means _____.
   a. Chaos
   b. Many languages
   c. Confusion
   d. Harmony

7. Satan wants to rule and reign _____.
   a. Over the Earth
   b. Taking the authority of man
   c. Taking the authority of Yeshua the Messiah
   d. All of the Above

ANSWERS

1. a
2. d
3. c
4. b
5. c
6. c
7. d

GRM BIBLE SCHOOL

REDISCOVERING GENESIS

UNIT 9

PART 4

Lesson 37

1. Lucifer is called _____.
   a. Star of the Morning
   b. Son of dawn
   c. King of Babylon and Tyre
   d. All of the above

2. Lucifer was created with precious _____ and gorgeous jewelry.
   a. Clay
   b. Rock
   c. Diamond
   d. Stones

3. The Lord establishes _____ as male and female.
   a. Satan
   b. Adam
   c. Eve
   d. None of the above

4. In order to get to Adam, Satan needed a _____ made of earth.
   a. Man
   b. Adam
   c. Both A and B
   d. Body

5. Psalms 8:5 "Yet You have made him a little lower than _____. And You crown him with glory and majesty."
   a. Angels
   b. God
   c. Satan
   d. None of the above

6. Man has authority over the angels as long as man is in righteous communion with _____.
   a. God
   b. Satan
   c. His neighbor
   d. The Angels

7. Satan wanted to have the image of the Almighty but couldn't because he wasn't _____ to be so.
   a. Made
   b. Created
   c. Existed
   d. Established

ANSWERS

1. d
2. d
3. b
4. d
5. b
6. a
7. b

GRM BIBLE SCHOOL

REDISCOVERING GENESIS

UNIT 9

PART 5

Lesson 38

1. Elohim made Adam higher than the _____.
    a. God
    b. Yeshua
    c. Angels
    d. None of the above

2. True or False: Satan does exist, and God has given us authority over him.
    a. True
    b. False

3. The woman should have asked "What spirit is speaking through the _____?" (Genesis 3:1-3)
    a. Satan
    b. Snake
    c. Adam
    d. None of the above

4. Every time we hear a voice or a thought or an idea or a doctrine that is contrary to the _____ of God, we actually are engaging with the snake in conversation.
    a. Word
    b. Creation
    c. Image and likeness
    d. None of the above

5. James 4:7 tells us how to achieve victory: "_____ therefore to God. Resist the devil and he will flee from you."
    a. Honor
    b. Give
    c. Sing
    d. Submit

6. If you hear, "Did God really say?" you know the _____ is talking.
   a. God
   b. Satan
   c. Angel
   d. Snake

7. 2 Chronicles 7:14 is the_____ to reverse what happened in the garden of Eden.
   a. Source
   b. Antidote
   c. Deception
   d. None of the Above

ANSWERS

1. c
2. a
3. b
4. a
5. d
6. d
7. b

GRM BIBLE SCHOOL

REDISCOVERING GENESIS

UNIT 9

PART 6

Lesson 39

1. True or False: The only way the devil can rule on earth is if he gets inside of a body.
   a. True
   b. False

2. KAVOD is the Hebrew word for "Glory", from the root meaning weighty or heavy. It represents:
   a. Thick Presence of God
   b. Wealth and Riches
   c. A and B above
   d. None of the above

3. From the moment man begins to hide from the presence of God, they will:
   a. Have fear and shame
   b. Be astute, shrewd, and manipulative
   c. Hide from the presence of God
   d. All of the above

4. It takes an act of God to:
   a. Commit sin
   b. Remove the nature of Satan
   c. Acquire the nature of God which is Yeshua the Messiah
   d. B and C above

5. Elohim is looking to see if there is anybody who will choose to _____ Him and His commandments.
   a. Reject
   b. Give
   c. Obey
   d. Curse

6. Yeshua came to _____ back the authority that we lost in the garden.
   a. Restore
   b. Delegate

    c.   Deny

    d.   None of the above

7. Yeshua said in Matthew 16:19: "I give you the _____ of the Kingdom."

    a.   Power

    b.   Rules

    c.   Keys

    d.   None of the Above

ANSWERS

1. a
2. c
3. d
4. d
5. c
6. a
7. c

GRM BIBLE SCHOOL

REDISCOVERING GENESIS

UNIT 9

PART 7

Lesson 40

1. Adam lost their authority to the snake: they _____ to the devil and sinned by breaking God's _____."
    a. Listened, commandments
    b. Ran, laws
    c. Gave, tablets
    d. None of the above

2. Nature of "Arum" is that man chooses to _____ and he says, "I am _____."
    a. Walk, strong
    b. Run, weak
    c. Hide, naked
    d. All of the above

3. Romans 6:23 states, "_____ have sinned and come short of the glory of God."
    a. Many
    b. All
    c. None
    d. Some

4. When we have excuses about our sin we are trying to _____ ourselves.
    a. Destroy
    b. Exalt
    c. Protect
    d. Cover

5. To be reconciled to God there has to be a _____ sacrifice.
    a. Human
    b. Animal
    c. Lamb
    d. Blood

6. We have to renounce and repent from _____ God's commandments.
    a. Obeying
    b. Restoring
    c. Breaking
    d. Honoring

7. God is looking for a man to _____, for He established that only man will rule over the earth.
    a. Walk
    b. Listen
    c. Rule
    d. Obey

ANSWERS

1. a
2. c
3. b
4. d
5. d
6. c
7. c

GRM BIBLE SCHOOL

REDISCOVERING GENESIS

UNIT 9

PART 8

Lesson 41

1. The first sacrifice is made for sin_____, an act of mercy, but was not eradication.
    a. Nature
    b. Covering
    c. Redemption
    d. History

2. The last sacrifice was about:
    a. Eradicating sin
    b. Removing the very nature of Satan from man
    c. A and B above
    d. None of the Above

3. Through Adam, sin and Satan's nature came in. Through Yeshua, sin goes out and the nature of _____ comes back in.
    a. Adam
    b. Prophets
    c. Angels
    d. God

4. Redemption means Man is totally back to his position of _____.
    a. Being in the likeness and image of the Creator
    b. Authority
    c. A and B above
    d. Freedom to live in sin nature

5. In the Old Covenant, we've got the sin covering. In the New Covenant we've got the sin _____ altogether.
    a. Removed
    b. Ignored
    c. Covered

d. Unveiled

6. Sin is an _____ - it is the very nature of _____.
   a. Equity, Satan
   b. Entity, Satan
   c. Enemy, Man
   d. None of the Above

7. Sin nature in man caused all creation to come under the _____. Creation is anxious for the sons of God to be _____.
   a. Curse, Revealed
   b. Chaos, Judged
   c. Groaning, Born
   d. Judgment, Destroyed

ANSWERS

1. b
2. c
3. d
4. c
5. a
6. b
7. a

GRM BIBLE SCHOOL

The Revival Cry of Josiah

Unit 10

GRM BIBLE SCHOOL

THE REVIVAL CRY OF JOSIAH

UNIT 10
PART 1

Lesson 42

1. According to 2 Kings 22:1, Josiah was 8 years old when he became _____.
   a. Prophet
   b. Priest
   c. King
   d. None of the Above

2. They find the book of the Law, the Manual of _____, under the Temple ruins.
   a. God
   b. Instructions
   c. Prophets
   d. None of the Above

3. Israel would not listen to the prophets who said "_____."
   a. Repent
   b. Enough
   c. Return
   d. None of the above

4. Josiah consults the prophetess Huldah: "What do we do with the Book of the _____? What is God saying?"
   a. Torah
   b. Manual
   c. Prophet
   d. Messiah

5. 2 Chronicles 7:14 states a promise from God: "If My people, who are called by My name, _____ (Surrender) themselves and pray and seek My face and turn from their wicked ways, then I will hear from heaven, I will forgive their sin and I will heal their land."
   a. Calm
   b. Ignore
   c. Humble

d. Turn

6. True or False: When Josiah heard the Book of the Torah read out loud, he did not realize that he had been breaking God's commandments.
   a. True
   b. False

7. Walking in intimacy with the Almighty is walking in obedience to His _____.
   a. Blessing
   b. Apostles
   c. Creed
   d. Commandments

ANSWERS

1. c
2. b
3. a
4. a
5. c
6. b
7. d

GRM BIBLE SCHOOL

THE REVIVAL CRY OF JOSIAH

UNIT 10

PART 2

Lesson 43

1. King Josiah repented: instead of experiencing _____, he experienced _____.
   a. Judgment, Revival
   b. Renewal, Revival
   c. Judgment, Condemnation
   d. None of the Above

2. Today nobody wants to endure a word that is a bit too _____.
   a. Weak
   b. Harsh
   c. Difficult
   d. All of the above

3. Josiah repented, went into mourning and, because he cried out from his heart, _____ heard him.
   a. Temple priests
   b. The people
   c. God
   d. None of the above

4. People get religious because they walk in _____ glory.
   a. Present
   b. Past
   c. Future
   d. Modern

5. Ba'al – anyone/anything that _____ you.
   a. Possesses
   b. Angers
   c. Loves
   d. Hates

6. Asherah – happiness (possessions _____ for happiness).
   a. Wanted
   b. Needed
   c. Gained
   d. None of the Above

7. "_____ therefore to God. Resist the devil and he will flee from you." (James 4:7)
   a. Surrender
   b. Come
   c. Go
   d. Submit

ANSWERS

1. a
2. b
3. c
4. b
5. a
6. b
7. d

GRM BIBLE SCHOOL

THE REVIVAL CRY OF JOSIAH

UNIT 10

PART 3

Lesson 44

1. Asherah – whatever you want to do or possess that makes you happy that is _____ to the commandments of God.
    a. Known
    b. Contrary
    c. Agreeable
    d. None of the above

2. The first thing we do when we hear the law, when we hear God's commandments, is _____ the Temple.
    a. Cleanse
    b. Decorate
    c. Fill
    d. Empty

3. Sanctify my _____, sanctify my mind, sanctify my body, O Adonai.
    a. Soul
    b. Spirit
    c. Ears
    d. Heart

4. God has given air and time for free, both to the righteous and to the _____ .
    a. Godly
    b. Creation
    c. Sinner
    d. None of the above

5. Meditate on the Word of God and the Laws of God and it will become _____ of you.
    a. Part
    b. None
    c. Completeness

d. All of the above

6. 1 John 1:9 states, "If we confess our sins, He is faithful and righteous to forgive us our sins and to _____ us from all unrighteousness."
   a. Remove
   b. Cleanse
   c. Wipe
   d. None of the Above

7. If you are hearing His voice, do not _____ your heart; surrender and let the Spirit of God come into your life.
   a. Harden
   b. Open
   c. Submit
   d. Surrender

ANSWERS

1. b
2. a
3. d
4. c
5. a
6. b
7. a

GRM BIBLE SCHOOL

THE REVIVAL CRY OF JOSIAH
UNIT 10
PART 4
Lesson 45

1. King Josiah would not be judged because he had been _____ before the Lord and he _____ his heart.
   a. Tender, Surrendered
   b. Cleansed, Emptied
   c. Open, Closed
   d. All of the above

2. Matthew 7:15-20 is a warning to beware of False Prophets. You will know them by their fruits; you cannot recognize whether people are true or false by their _____.
   a. Money
   b. Gifts
   c. Church name
   d. None of the Above

3. A healing or preaching that doesn't bring repentance will only bring _____ healing.
   a. Positive
   b. Complete
   c. Superficial
   d. Lasting

4. Why a superficial healing? The word preached did not demand repentance or demand a _____ lifestyle.
   a. Change in
   b. Happy
   c. Carefree
   d. None of the above

5. May we hear the word of a true prophet that:
   a. Causes us to repent
   b. Removes idolatries from our life
   c. Brings revival instead of judgment

d. All of the above

6. True or False: Balaam knew that he could not curse the Israelites, for they are a blessed people. He also could not add anything to the Word of the Lord.

   a. True
   b. False

7. "He who turns his _____ from listening to the Law, even his prayer is an abomination." (Prov. 28:9)

   a. Heart
   b. Nose
   c. Eye
   d. Ear

ANSWERS

1. a
2. b
3. c
4. a
5. d
6. a
7. d

GRM BIBLE SCHOOL

THE REVIVAL CRY OF JOSIAH

UNIT 10

PART 5

Lesson 46

1. Josiah began to rebuild the _____ of the Lord and establish back the holy worship.
   a. Word
   b. Temple
   c. Torah
   d. Foundation

2. We are in the season between revival and _____.
   a. Judgment
   b. Truth
   c. Fire
   d. Repentance

3. The key for _____ during the time of Josiah was to find the lost book, hear the word of the law and be willing to do what it said.
   a. Battle
   b. Revival
   c. Acceptance
   d. None of the Above

4. Today judgment is being poured out in the House of the _____ and in the _____.
   a. Lord, Nations
   b. Fishermen, Nations
   c. Israelites, Church
   d. All of the above

5. When we talk about the early Church we talk about a _____ Church.
   a. Roman
   b. Pagan
   c. Greek
   d. Jewish

6. From the 4th Century the Hebrew Holy Scriptures was called "_____" Testament.
   a. New
   b. Old
   c. Greek
   d. Jewish

7. The entire Word of God is established in Heaven and it _____ be removed. (Psalms 119:89)
   a. Can
   b. Cannot
   c. Will
   d. Should

ANSWERS

1. b
2. a
3. b
4. a
5. d
6. b
7. b

GRM BIBLE SCHOOL

THE REVIVAL CRY OF JOSIAH

UNIT 10
PART 6

Lesson 47

---

1. True or False: The key for revival at that time (of Josiah) is going to be the key for this time as well.
   a. True
   b. False

2. The Book of the Law was _____ under the ruins of the Temple.
   a. Never
   b. Destroyed
   c. Hidden
   d. Written

3. God says the only way to find rest is to look to the _____ paths.
   a. Lost
   b. Ancient
   c. New
   d. Renewed

4. The Holy Spirit's main role is to be our Torah Teacher: To lead us in the laws and commandments of God - To lead us into all _____.
   a. Truth
   b. Directions
   c. Paths
   d. None of the Above

5. The New Covenant is described in Jeremiah 31:31-33 - "I will make a new covenant with the house of _____ and with the house of Judah."
   a. Rome
   b. Israel
   c. Josiah
   d. Ephraim

6. For salvation is of the _____. (John 4:22)
   a. Gentiles
   b. Greeks
   c. Jews
   d. Church

7. When we begin to accept that the foundations of the faith are _____, from that moment revival begins. (Romans 11:15)
   a. New Testament
   b. Roman
   c. Egyptian
   d. Hebrew

ANSWERS

1. a
2. c
3. b
4. a
5. b
6. c
7. d

GRM BIBLE SCHOOL

Son of Man Revealed

Unit 11

GRM BIBLE SCHOOL

SON OF MAN REVEALED

UNIT 11

PART 1

Lesson 48

1. Romans 8:19 states that the creation is longing for the sons of God to be revealed, to get out of the _____ to which it has been subjected.
    a. Lawlessness
    b. Corruption
    c. Bondage
    d. Strongholds

2. Sin means to _____ God's commandments.
    a. Break
    b. Obey
    c. Honor
    d. Love

3. If you do not know Him, you are not catalogued as being in the _____ Covenant.
    a. Old
    b. Ancient
    c. New
    d. Holy

4. True freedom is holiness, righteousness, purity, and _____ to God's commandments.
    a. Disobedience
    b. Obedience
    c. Rejection
    d. None of the Above

5. Man, possessed of the sin nature of Satan, has been ruling on the earth and the earth has been_____ with immorality.
    a. Filled
    b. Cleansed
    c. Content

        d. All of the above

6. When you are truly born again, you have no more desire for _____.
    a. Righteousness
    b. Sin
    c. Peace
    d. Joy

7. Knowing the Lord means to walk in _____ and to walk in obedience to the commandments.
    a. Righteousness
    b. Darkness
    c. Lawlessness
    d. None of the above

ANSWERS

1. b
2. a
3. c
4. b
5. a
6. b
7. a

GRM BIBLE SCHOOL

SON OF MAN REVEALED

UNIT 11

PART 2

LESSON 49

---

1. God says that this is the New Covenant: I will put My laws in their _____ and in their minds. I will forgive their sin.
    a. Souls
    b. Mouth
    c. Hearts
    d. None of the Above

2. The Gentiles have to join in the pre-existing covenant that is renewed with _____.
    a. The Church
    b. Israel
    c. Gentiles
    d. All of the Above

3. Everything connected with _____ the commandments is a sign of the New Covenant. (I John 2)
    a. Obedience to
    b. Disobedience to
    c. Rejecting
    d. Opposing

4. Matthew 7:21 states, "Not everyone who says to Me, 'Lord, Lord', will _____ the kingdom of heaven, but he who does the will of My Father who is in heaven will enter."
    a. Join
    b. Enter
    c. Receive
    d. None of the Above

5. Lawlessness means we break God's commandments and think _____ of it.
    a. Well
    b. Good
    c. Nothing

    d. Something

6. In Matthew 5:13-20 Yeshua said, "I did not come to _____ but to fulfill". This means we should walk like He walked.
    a. Abolish
    b. Judge
    c. Condemn
    d. None of the Above

7. If we compare the New Covenant with the Old Covenant, it is _____. This makes us realize we must have the Holy Spirit.
    a. Easier
    b. Harder
    c. Good
    d. All of the Above

ANSWERS

1. c
2. b
3. a
4. b
5. c
6. a
7. b

GRM BIBLE SCHOOL

Radical Lifestyle

Unit 12

GRM BIBLE SCHOOL

RADICAL LIFESTYLE

UNIT 12

PART 1

Lesson 50

1. "The one who says he abides in Him ought himself to walk in the _____ _____ as He walked." (1 John 2:6)
    a. Same manner
    b. Opposite manner
    c. New Covenant
    d. Old Covenant

2. True or False: The early church had a radical lifestyle; they understood that Yeshua came to show us the way to walk in His commandments.
    a. True
    b. False

3. Gods Army: In the early Church people signed up at the first booth and realized their lives _____.
    a. Would not change
    b. Were not their own
    c. Would be happy every day
    d. All of the above

4. Yeshua is tremendously _____.
    a. Unhappy
    b. Unloving
    c. Loving
    d. Ungrateful

5. Matthew 5:20 states, "For I say to you that unless your righteousness surpasses that of the scribes and the Pharisees, you will not _____ the kingdom of heaven.
    a. Enter
    b. Join
    c. See
    d. None of the Above

6. There will not be an End Time Revival unless the Church _____.
   a. Returns
   b. Repents
   c. Forgives
   d. Rejoices

7. God is calling us to _____ (Yadah) Him.
   a. Choose
   b. Deny
   c. Know
   d. Reject

ANSWERS

1. a
2. a
3. b
4. c
5. a
6. b
7. c

GRM BIBLE SCHOOL

RADICAL LIFESTYLE

UNIT 12
PART 2

Lesson 51

1. The Early Church's radical lifestyle came from a _____ of God, which led them to do _____ things.
    a. Fear, Unrighteous
    b. Fear, Righteous
    c. Mistrust, Unrighteous
    d. None of the Above

2. In Matthew 5:17 we hear Yeshua state, "Do not think that I came to abolish the Law or the Prophets; I did not come to abolish but to _____."
    a. Redeem
    b. Remove
    c. Fulfill
    d. Destroy

3. In regards to the Hebrew Holy Scriptures, we read in 2 Timothy 3:15-17 that "all Scripture" is inspired by _____."
    a. God
    b. Man
    c. Adam
    d. Satan

4. The New Testament portions of the scripture were not canonized until the _____.
    a. 1st Century
    b. 2nd Century
    c. 3rd Century
    d. 4th Century

5. Many accept the Lord, but there is _____ _____ in their lives.
    a. No Change
    b. Much Change
    c. Tremendous Change

d. Little Change

6. Many people are so lost and keep _____ the same mistakes because they refuse to hear the commandments of God.
   a. Repeating
   b. Fearing
   c. Desiring
   d. None of the above

7. The _____ for breaking the commandments repeats themselves to the 3rd and 4th generation. (Exodus 20:5)
   a. Blessings
   b. Curse
   c. Pain
   d. All of the Above

ANSWERS

1. b
2. c
3. a
4. d
5. a
6. a
7. b

GRM BIBLE SCHOOL

RADICAL LIFESTYLE

UNIT 12

PART 3

Lesson 52

1. John 2:7 states, "Beloved I am not writing a new commandment to you, but an old commandment which you have heard from the _____; the old commandment is the word which you have heard."
    a. Prophets
    b. Apostles
    c. Beginning
    d. None of the Above

2. How many have read the whole book, the commandments and the instructions, and asked the Holy Spirit to write it in their _____?
    a. Mind
    b. Heart
    c. Forehead
    d. Hand

3. A radical lifestyle is a lifestyle of _____, _____, and _____.
    a. Holiness, Righteousness, Obedience
    b. Unholiness, Righteousness, Disobedience
    c. Righteousness, Obedience, Disobedience
    d. All of the Above

4. Holy means separated unto God, not for _____ use.
    a. Personal
    b. Own
    c. Common
    d. None of the Above

5. Yeshua said, "Do not think that I have come to bring _____ on this earth." (Luke 12:51)
    a. Love
    b. Joy
    c. A and B above

    d. Peace

6. In Rome, the early Church was under terrible _____.
    a. Teachings
    b. Divisions
    c. Persecution
    d. Poverty

7. True or False: The peace that believers acquired from Constantine over 1600 years ago cost the Church little.
    a. True
    b. False

ANSWERS

1. c
2. b
3. a
4. c
5. d
6. c
7. b

GRM BIBLE SCHOOL

RADICAL LIFESTYLE

UNIT 12

PART 4

Lesson 53

1. Constantine's decree: "On the Venerable Day of the _____ let the magistrates and people residing in cities rest, and let all workshops be closed."
    a. Passover
    b. Moon
    c. Stars
    d. Sun

2. Revelation 5:1-5 states, "….the Lion that is from the tribe of _____, the Root of David, has overcome so as to open the book and its seven seals."
    a. Benjamin
    b. Simeon
    c. Levi
    d. Judah

3. True or False: The gospel of peace says, "Make peace at any cost".
    a. True
    b. False

4. False _____ always causes us to surrender to the enemy and relinquish our territory.
    a. Joy
    b. Happiness
    c. Love
    d. Peace

5. Preaching the _____ roots of the faith to the Church is a matter of life and death.
    a. Jewish
    b. Roman
    c. Pagan
    d. Catholic

6. Every spirit that does not recognize the Jewishness of the Messiah is the spirit of _____. (I John 4:3)
   a. Greece
   b. Anti-Messiah
   c. Paganism
   d. Messiah

7. A gospel of peace instead of the Gospel of Shalom is a _____ grace gospel instead of the Eternal Gospel – it is an Anti-Messiah _____.
   a. Cheap, Spirit
   b. Pure, Spirit
   c. True, Spirit
   d. None of the Above

ANSWERS

1. d
2. d
3. a
4. d
5. a
6. b
7. a

GRM BIBLE SCHOOL

RADICAL LIFESTYLE

UNIT 12

PART 5

LESSON 54

1. God is calling us to a radical lifestyle with no compromise and _____ obedience.
    a. Complete
    b. Some
    c. Occasional
    d. All of the Above

2. According to Daniel 1:9, Daniel made up his mind that he would not _____ himself while living in Babylon.
    a. Defile
    b. Destroy
    c. Condemn
    d. Deny

3. Daniel feared God above the _____, above the desire to _____ his life.
    a. Law, Improve
    b. King, Save
    c. Magicians, Preserve
    d. None of the Above

4. Daniel was willing to risk his life not to _____ the Lord's commandments.
    a. Protect
    b. Guard
    c. Keep
    d. Break

5. Matthew 5:17-19 states, "Whoever _____ and teaches (His commandments), he shall be called great in the kingdom of heaven."
    a. Keeps
    b. Breaks
    c. Disobeys

d. Rejects

6. During the Spanish Inquisition Jews forced to convert to Catholicism had to eat pork to prove their conversion and had to profane and desecrate the _____.
   a. Shabbat (Sabbath)
   b. Temple
   c. Scriptures
   d. Priests

7. Despite the threat of punishment, this is written about Daniel: "He continued kneeling on his knees three times a day, _____ and giving thanks before his God." (Daniel 6:6)
   a. Singing
   b. Praying
   c. Trusting
   d. None of the Above

ANSWERS

1. a
2. a
3. b
4. d
5. a
6. a
7. b

GRM BIBLE SCHOOL

RADICAL LIFESTYLE

UNIT 12

PART 6

Lesson 55

1. Daniel was a righteous man who walked with God. He would not break God's commandments even if it meant losing his_____.
    a. Mind
    b. Life
    c. Position
    d. Money

2. To stand with _____ can cause you to be persecuted.
    a. Rome
    b. Israel
    c. America
    d. All of the above

3. During a trial in Daniel 6:16-22 we hear these words spoken to Daniel: "Your God whom you constantly serve will Himself _____ you."
    a. Destroy
    b. Consume
    c. Abandon
    d. Deliver

4. Just before the Council of Nicaea, most of the believers were _____.
    a. Jews
    b. Gentile
    c. Pagan
    d. None of the Above

5. God wants us to be like Daniel: _____ in our faith and bold in our radical lifestyle of righteousness.
    a. Timid
    b. Fearful
    c. Bold

149

d. Weak

6. True or False: If we are found righteous before Him, if we are found pure and innocent before Him, He will shut the mouths of the lions.
   a. True
   b. False

7. Those that are walking carefully and _____ God's commandments and are putting God first, without fear of man, they will be protected.
   a. Reject
   b. Nullify
   c. Refuse
   d. Obey

ANSWERS

1. b
2. b
3. d
4. b
5. c
6. a
7. d

GRM BIBLE SCHOOL

Discovering the Hebrew Scriptures

Reading Schedule

1. Yeshua is the Name
2. Stormy Weather
3. Eradicating the Cancer of Religion
4. Restoration of Holy Giving

BOOK 1

Yeshua Is The Name

1. Yeshua (commonly called Jesus Christ) is the real Hebrew name for the Jewish Messiah. In Hebrew, Yeshua means:
   a. Lamb of God
   b. King of Kings
   c. Salvation, deliverance and redemption
   d. One who heals

2. Yeshua is the "Torah made flesh" or the _____ Torah. As you follow Him, and His Ruach HaKodesh (Holy Spirit) He will lead you to the Truth.
   a. Old
   b. New
   c. Last
   d. Living

3. True or False: Yeshua will not return until all things are restored (Acts 3:19-21). Among "all things," one of the most important ones—if not the greatest one—is the restoration of His holy name.
   a. True
   b. False

4. The Council of Nicaea divorced the church from everything _____, even from the real Jewish

name of the Messiah.
- a. Catholic
- b. Jewish
- c. Unholy
- d. Pagan

5. Many believers know that the real name of the Messiah is Yeshua, but they do not understand the life and death importance of _____ and restoring His holy name.
   - a. Repenting
   - b. Hearing
   - c. Writing
   - d. Speaking

6. Jesus is a form of the name Iesous, which is derived from Ieso, and can be traced back to _____ worship.
   - a. Holy
   - b. Moon
   - c. Sun
   - d. All of the above

7. No one has the right to change the name given by Elohim Himself through His Angel _____.
   - a. Michael
   - b. Gabriel
   - c. Lucifer
   - d. Raphael

8. Christianity, as we know it today, was born in Rome under the Roman Empire; the church needs to change her focus from Rome to _____.
   - a. Greece
   - b. America
   - c. Constantinople
   - d. Jerusalem

9. Just as it was with Yoseph (Joseph), whose identity was hidden from his brothers behind an Egyptian name, the Jewish people will NOT recognize their Brother and _____ when He is introduced to them as Jesus Christ, the Christian God.
   - a. Messiah
   - b. Friend
   - c. Family
   - d. None of the above

10. Yeshua is in heaven right now, but His bride is on the earth; the only way that He can reveal Himself to Israel is through a heart-circumcised bride that displays the _____ of the gospel and carries the

name of Yeshua and not Jesus Christ!
a. Symbols
b. Jewishness
c. Hypocrisy
d. All of the above

ANSWERS

1. c   2. d   3. a   4. b   5. a   6. c   7. b   8. d   9. a   10. b

GRM BIBLE SCHOOL

BOOK 2

STORMY WEATHER

1. The Almighty consistently speaks His _____ to man through weather.
   a. Will
   b. Word
   c. Judgments
   d. Commandments

2. Two factors will be used by Yahveh for judgment upon nations: a) obedience to His laws and commandments (written or spoken) and b) how they have treated _____ and the Jewish people.
   a. Israel
   b. Egypt
   c. Rabbis
   d. Priests

3. Stormy weather creating catastrophes is judgment, according to Isaiah 34:8 which states it is "_____ for the cause of Zion."
   a. Judgment
   b. Recompense
   c. Disaster
   d. Coincidence

4. True or False: An Esther Church will arise, full of authority and much power, displaying His glory and bringing forth the End Time harvest of nations.
   a. True
   b. False

5. As the fire that burns the forest, as the flame that sets the mountains on fire, so pursue them with Your tempest, terrify them with Your storm. Fill their faces with confusion, that they may seek Your name, Yahveh. (Psalm 83) The writer of this Psalm seems to be well aware of the use of winds, storms and tempests as an _____.
   a. Indication of sin
   b. Instrument of Yahveh's judgment
   c. Evil omen
   d. Ordinary natural occurrence

6. Woe unto that nation or people that judges and deals with the _____ people in a hostile way; the highways of history are littered with the remains of nations who were hostile to them.
   a. Poor
   b. Rich
   c. Jewish
   d. Gentile

7. Fully backed by the U.S. government, the Gaza withdrawal displaced all Jewish residents and was completed on August 23, 2005. That same day Hurricane _____ formed, soon striking with devastating force making landfall at New Orleans, displacing hundreds of thousands of Americans and costing over $150 billion in damage.
   a. Andrew
   b. Katrina
   c. Irma
   d. None of the above

8. YAHVEH is about to _____ the world for rejecting His Son, whom He sent, and for rejecting His ways and Holy Commandments, for rejecting His People Israel - the Jewish people, and for dividing their land.
   a. Judge
   b. Save
   c. Love
   d. Reward

9. Any holy child of God, who is walking in obedience to Yeshua, has the _____ to cast out unclean spirits and stop all unauthorized storms. The key factor is "Walking in obedience to Yeshua" which is a holy walk.
   a. Knowledge
   b. Choice
   c. Decision
   d. Authority

10. Judgment must first begin in the House of Yah before revival can come, and the first ones to be judged are the_____: those who have been prophesying falsely, the soothsayers that caress the ears of the flock and those that lead the people astray with false teaching that does not produce righteousness, holiness and devotion to the Most High!
    a. Teachers
    b. Wicked and Unbelievers
    c. Priests and the Prophets
    d. Believers

ANSWERS

1. c   2. a   3. b   4. a   5. b   6. c   7. b   8. a   9. d   10. c

GRM BIBLE SCHOOL

BOOK 3

Eradicating the Cancer of Religion

1. True or False: All people are religious, in one way or another; we all worship something or other apart from an intimate personal relationship with The Creator.
   a. True
   b. False

2. The author's definition of Religion: the human quest for knowledge, protection, provision, self-improvement and satisfaction _____ a personal, intimate relationship with the Creator.
   a. Including
   b. In addition to
   c. Outside of
   d. All of the above

3. From the beginning, Elohim, the Creator, desired Adam (man and woman) to know Him only – and to know everything else through Him, through His eyes, and not in an _____ fashion (outside the personal relationship with Him - using the 'Tree of Knowledge', reason and logic).
   a. Arrogant
   b. Humble
   c. Dependent
   d. Independent

4. Idolatry is the foundation of every religious system and idolatry is fueled by _____. (Gen. 3:6)
   a. Jealousy
   b. Lust
   c. Knowledge
   d. Scripture

5. All religions and cults (and, of course, the Occult and New Age) are based on a quest of knowledge in order to obtain power _____.
   a. Apart from God
   b. And favor
   c. To rule
   d. And fame

6. The essence of all religious systems is _____ without intimacy or obedience to the Lord of the

Universe, YHVH – Elohim.
- a. Repentance
- b. Praising
- c. Tithing
- d. Sacrifice

7. The Temple sacrificial system involved blood that covered sin, but it did not FREE man from sin; Romans 5:8 tells us about the _____ of the Father, demonstrated through His own Son Yeshua's sacrifice of blood shed for us – this truly sets us free, but it requires us to have faith (believe).
   - a. Love
   - b. Will
   - c. Mind
   - d. Hope

8. Our Jewish Messiah is Yeshua (the Hebrew name for Jesus Christ) - His name Yeshua means _____.
   - a. Joyful
   - b. Peace
   - c. Love
   - d. Salvation

9. All religious systems work on the deathly foundation of disbelieving God and His _____, which brings about independence from Him and religion that always causes murder.
   - a. Prophets
   - b. Apostles
   - c. Word
   - d. Children

10. _____ religious systems are based on "what man can do"; God's salvation through Yeshua has nothing to do with man's intervention because He was not murdered. (John 10:17,18)
    - a. Some
    - b. All
    - c. A few
    - d. None of the above

ANSWERS

1. a   2. c   3. d   4. b   5. a   6. d   7. a   8. d   9. c   10. b

GRM BIBLE SCHOOL

BOOK 4

Restoration of the Holy Giving

1. True or False: Wrong giving or lack of prescribed giving (such as tithes, first fruits and Feast offerings) can incur a terrible curse and is the number one issue of repentance before revival can come.
   a. True
   b. False

2. The _____ offering is an offering of honor to YHVH (according to Proverbs 3:9,10); when we give this offering to Elohim's ministers that are assigned to bless us, it is Elohim Himself that we are honoring in that Minister.
   a. Feast
   b. First Fruits
   c. Tithe
   d. None of the above

3. The Whole Tithe (Malachi 3:8-10) is 10% of all your income _____ you pay bills and debts.
   a. Before
   b. After
   c. Before or after
   d. None of the above

4. We must _____ the sin of withholding First Fruits and Tithes to those that have mentored and taught us the Word and not only to YHVH.
   a. Remember
   b. Hide
   c. Confess
   d. Share

5. There are three categories of tithes, including The First Tithe, The Third Year Tithe and The Feast Tithe. Which one is shared between the Levites, the widow, the orphan and the stranger?
   a. The First Tithe
   b. The Third Year Tithe
   c. The Feast Tithe
   d. Both A & C above

6. The restoration of the true _____ Ministry needs to lead to a place of abundance and blessing

where no one lacks anything. (Acts 4:32-35)
   a. Priestly
   b. Prophetic
   c. Pastoral
   d. Apostolic

7. The Feast Tithe enables you to come up to _____.
   a. The altar
   b. Higher Ground
   c. Zion
   d. Prosperity

8. Start putting aside all of your tithes: The First (to the Levites), The Second (Feasts in Jerusalem) and The Third (3% for the poor and needy) and you will see a shift in your spiritual wellbeing that will be followed by your _____ wellbeing as well.
   a. Mental
   b. Physical
   c. Financial
   d. None of the above

9. Proverbs 11:4 uses the Hebrew word Zedaka meaning "righteousness" which delivers from death – it should have been better translated as "_____" which delivers from death.
   a. Righteous giving
   b. Holiness
   c. Repentance
   d. Salvation

10. When you sow a potent _____ out of extravagant love and faith or out of extravagant obedience, you will never go unnoticed. Do not let fear stop you from fruitfulness and multiplication.
    a. Offering
    b. Seed
    c. Word
    d. None of the above

ANSWERS

1. a   2. b   3. a   4. c   5. b   6. d   7. c   8. c   9. a   10. b

GRM BIBLE SCHOOL

FOUNDATIONS OF FAITH REVEALED

Term Paper

INSTRUCTIONS

In four pages to ten pages, discuss what you have learned through Lessons 34-55 and the four books by Archbishop Dominiquae Bierman. Make sure to include the following points:

1. Discuss what happened between Genesis 1:1 and Genesis 1:2

2. Discuss Satan, his nature, and how it has, and still does, affect the world.

3. Trace the central theme of repentance from Genesis through living a radical lifestyle.

4. Both the story of Josiah and the story of Daniel help explain why there is so little power in the Church today when compared to the early Church.

5. What Yeshua came to do and His relationship and attitude with the laws and commandments of God.

6. *Extra*: Matthew 12:1-13 – Yeshua is accused of breaking the law. If Yeshua never broke the laws and commandments of His father, how do you account for these accusations?

Make sure to cite all references. Biblical references need book, chapter, and verse. For example: Isaiah 53:4-6. Book references for Archbishop's books need title and page number. Use quotation marks for direct quotes. Other material cite appropriately.

FORMAT

- Double spaced with 12pt font
- Your Name
- Title as, "Discovering the Hebrew Scriptures Term Paper"
- Summary: This is a one paragraph summary of your term paper.
- Main Section: Make sure it has a logical flow with an introduction, main body, and conclusion.
- Practical Application: This is a separate section at the end. Include what have you learned and how you can use this information or how it can be applied in these End-times. Include any new insights you may have.

GRM ISRAELI BIBLE SCHOOL
LEVEL 3: HEBREW SCRIPTURES RESTORED

STUDENT WORKBOOK

UNITS 13-19

www.grmbibleschool.com

info@grmbibleschool.com

GRM BIBLE SCHOOL

The Enemies of God

Unit 13

GRM BIBLE SCHOOL

THE ENEMIES OF GOD

UNIT 13

PART 1

LESSON 56

1. According to 1 Peter 4:17 Judgment must begin in the House of _____.
   a. Israel
   b. God
   c. Ephraim
   d. Judah

2. YHVH - The name of _____ - I AM
   a. Jesus
   b. Aaron
   c. Moses
   d. God

3. When we talk about the Father, we see His dealing with _____ as the God of _____ and the God of _____.
   a. Israel, Judgment, Law
   b. Judah, Judgment, Law
   c. Gentiles, Judgement, Law
   d. None of the Above

4. Both the God of mercy and the God of _____ is our Father.
   a. Truth
   b. Love
   c. Judgment
   d. None of the Above

5. When we cry out for revival we are crying out for an attack of _____ on society.
   a. Satan
   b. Angels
   c. God
   d. All of the above

6. In the days of Noah, everyone was God's enemy except _____ and his family.
   a. Moses
   b. Noah
   c. Both A and B
   d. None of the Above

7. True or False: An enemy of God hates God's laws; a friend of God will love His laws.
   a. True
   b. False

ANSWERS

1. b
2. d
3. a
4. c
5. c
6. b
7. a

GRM BIBLE SCHOOL

THE ENEMIES OF GOD

UNIT 13

PART 2

Lesson 57

1. God's _____ are not always popular. God's _____ are always popular.
   a. Friends, Sons
   b. Friends, Enemies
   c. Enemies, People
   d. People, Children

2. Those having a carnal mind are in hostility with _____. (Romans 8:7) James 4:4-6 also tells us that those who are friends with the _____ are enemies of God.
   a. God, World
   b. Man, World
   c. Satan, World
   d. None of the above

3. Anyone willing to sell his calling to God, his walk with God, in order to satisfy a carnal desire is an_____ of God.
   a. Friend
   b. Enemy
   c. Son
   d. All of the above

4. Esau could have received the birthright, but lost the possibility of becoming a _____ nation, of having a great and famous name, and of being _____ financially and spiritually.
   a. Great, Blessed
   b. Famous, Cursed
   c. Great, Cursed
   d. Cursed, Blessed

5. People like Esau don't think of the _____ glory; they want their needs met now.
   a. Past
   b. Future
   c. Present

    d. None of the above

6. Many Christians today don't believe in the amazing calling to be a _____ in the world (Philippians 2:15) - we are called to represent Yeshua the Messiah here on this earth.
    a. Light
    b. Friend
    c. Judge
    d. None of the Above

7. According to James 3:1 we learn that those who teach the Word are _____ more severely.
    a. Honored
    b. Judged
    c. Liked
    d. Loved

ANSWERS

1. b
2. a
3. b
4. a
5. b
6. a
7. b

GRM BIBLE SCHOOL

THE ENEMIES OF GOD

UNIT 13

PART 3

Lesson 58

1. Birthright carries all the _____ and _____ of the family.
   a. Authority, Curses
   b. Curses, Authority
   c. Blessings, Authority
   d. None of the above

2. Two Spirits are represented by Esau and Jacob: One is willing to _____ the need - the other is willing to _____ his soul for the need.
   a. Fast, Sell
   b. Trade, Sell
   c. Give, Sell
   d. All of the Above

3. Romans 6:23 states, "For the wages of sin is _____."
   a. Life
   b. Death
   c. Evil
   d. All of the above

4. Whatever we hear gets into our minds and gets into our heart – so we are told in Holy Scripture, "Today if you hear His voice, do not harden your _____." (Hebrew 3:15)
   a. Souls
   b. Minds
   c. Hearts
   d. Desires

5. Constantine brought the spirit of Esau into the _____.
   a. World
   b. Church
   c. Earth

d. Both A and B

6. True or False: The calling of God carries the testing, the trials, and the suffering so that we may know Him in His suffering and in the power of His resurrection.
   a. True
   b. False

7. The purpose of Esau's life was to be _____; the purpose of Jacob's life was to do the will of God.
   a. Whole
   b. Complete
   c. Gratified
   d. All of the Above

ANSWERS

1. c
2. a
3. b
4. c
5. b
6. a
7. c

GRM BIBLE SCHOOL

THE ENEMIES OF GOD

UNIT 13

PART 4

Lesson 59

1. In these end times it is necessary to know who are the friends of God and who are enemies of God. It is time to become _____ about our own lives and the people around us.
    a. Violent
    b. Discerning
    c. Judgmental
    d. All of the above

2. If there has not been a radical change since you accepted the LORD, you have not accepted or been _____ to the Gospel of Yeshua.
    a. Obedient
    b. Listening
    c. Hearing
    d. None of the Above

3. In 1 Samuel 2:12-17 we see that the sons of Eli were _____ (belial) men; thus the _____ of the young men was very great before the LORD, for the men despised the offering of the LORD.
    a. Worthless, Act
    b. Worthless, Sin
    c. Hopeless, Sin
    d. None of the Above

4. Eli's sons officiated as priests even though they were _____ and idolatrous.
    a. Pure
    b. Holy
    c. Immoral
    d. Clean

5. Eli's mistake was that he allowed the sin to go on. If we allow the sin in our congregation to go on, we become exactly like _____.
    a. Eli
    b. Satan

c. Adam

d. None of the above

6. We are told in 1 Corinthians 5:1-2 that any saint of God who refuses to repent from his sin needs to be removed from our midst.

    a. True

    b. False

7. From his actions we can see that Eli wanted to honor his _____ more than God.

    a. Relatives

    b. Friends

    c. Daughters

    d. Sons

ANSWERS

1. b

2. a

3. b

4. c

5. a

6. a

7. d

GRM BIBLE SCHOOL

THE ENEMIES OF GOD

UNIT 13

PART 5

Lesson 60

1. From James 4:6 we learn that friendship with the world means you are an _____ of God.
   a. Friend
   b. Enemy
   c. Child
   d. Son

2. An unrighteous priest perverts the entire _____.
   a. Land
   b. Country
   c. Congregation
   d. Nation

3. Today the church is filled with immoral people who call themselves Christians, but we are dishonoring God if we call ourselves believers and walk like the _____ .
   a. Priest
   b. Devil
   c. Saint
   d. None of the above

4. Before we lose the glory altogether there is a need for _____.
   a. Teaching
   b. Preaching
   c. Cleansing
   d. None of the above

5. In 1 Samuel 2:29 God said to Eli, "you have honored your sons above God so God will dishonor _____."
   a. Man
   b. Woman
   c. You

d. Them

6. A Samuel generation is one that is fully dedicated to the living God and wants the _____ of God, walking in His _____ commandments.
   a. Presence, Righteous
   b. Presence, Unrighteous
   c. Hands, Righteous
   d. None of the Above

7. We are at the time of _____ because of immorality, perversion, and idolatry in the camp.
   a. Repentance
   b. Righteousness
   c. Wickedness
   d. None of the Above

ANSWERS

1. b
2. c
3. b
4. c
5. c
6. a
7. a

GRM BIBLE SCHOOL

THE ENEMIES OF GOD

UNIT 13

PART 6

Lesson 61

1. In the Church today there is _____ of glory because of sin and unrighteousness.
   a. Plenty
   b. Fullness
   c. Lack
   d. Abundance

2. The presence of God needs to be handled by righteous priests that _____ God.
   a. Dishonor
   b. Disrespect
   c. Obey
   d. Reject

3. 2 Samuel 6:6 illustrates a principle: When the Presence of God wants to fall, let it _____.
   a. In
   b. Fall
   c. Die
   d. Disappear

4. True or False: We cannot cry out for God's presence without receiving more of God's Word, His Character, and His Ways.
   a. True
   b. False

5. God is not calling us to satisfy _____ desires and needs.
   a. Our
   b. Their
   c. His
   d. All of the above

6. Samuel in Hebrew is Shmuel, meaning "One that hears what _____ has to say."
   a. Satan

b. God

c. Prophet

d. None of the above

7. 1 Samuel 7:1-17 tells us that when we have righteous priests we will _____ the enemy, but when we have unrighteous priests we are not victorious.

   a. Defeat

   b. Serve

   c. Fear

   d. None of the Above

ANSWERS

1. c
2. c
3. b
4. a
5. a
6. b
7. a

GRM BIBLE SCHOOL

THE ENEMIES OF GOD

UNIT 13

PART 7

Lesson 62

1. King Saul became another _____ of God.
    a. Friend
    b. Enemy
    c. Son
    d. None of the above

2. Saul needed to follow some instructions, some strategies that the living _____ had given Samuel.
    a. Priest
    b. God
    c. Eli
    d. All of the above

3. Saul wanted the crowd more than the _____ of the crowd.
    a. Man
    b. Jesus
    c. Lord
    d. None of the Above

4. It is important to know what is our motivation: it must be to give glory to _____ and not to get fame for _____.
    a. God, Ourselves
    b. Satan, Ourselves
    c. Ourselves, God
    d. Both B and C

5. Saul didn't _____, therefore he lost the kingdom.
    a. Believe
    b. Honor
    c. Repent
    d. Listen

6. 1 Samuel 13:13-14 states, "You have acted foolishly, you have _____ _____ the commandments of the Lord your God."
   a. Not Kept
   b. Not Disobeyed
   c. Not Refused
   d. Not Heard

7. We are reminded in 1 Samuel 15:22 that God demands absolute _____, just as in John 14:15 we read, "If you love Me, keep My Commandments".
   a. Disobedience
   b. Obedience
   c. Rebellion
   d. Honor

ANSWERS

1. b
2. b
3. c
4. a
5. c
6. a
7. b

GRM BIBLE SCHOOL

THE ENEMIES OF GOD

UNIT 13

PART 8

Lesson 63

1. King Saul _____ his kingdom because he loved his position a lot more than he loved God.
    a. Saved
    b. Lost
    c. Guarded
    d. Protected

2. Psalms 83:1-8 shows us how nations join against Israel, but we know the only politics that will stand will be Biblical politics. God is going to keep _____ promises no matter what.
    a. His
    b. Their
    c. United
    d. Gentile

3. For the most part, the nations around Israel _____ Israel to the point of even obliterating the name.
    a. Love
    b. Honor
    c. Respect
    d. Hate

4. The Romans changed the name of Israel to_____.
    a. Edom
    b. Sodom
    c. Moab
    d. Palestine

5. The purpose of the Fatah, PLO, Hamas, Hezbollah is the "Final Solution" (extermination) concerning _____.
    a. Israel
    b. Jordan
    c. Syria

d. Samaria

6. A Jewish National home was to be established by the Balfour Declaration of 1917, which includes Israel of today and _____ of today.

    a. Jordan

    b. Syria

    c. Lebanon

    d. Palestine

7. Whoever is an enemy of Israel is _____ of God, detailed by Zechariah 2:8 - "For thus says the Lord of Hosts, after glory He has sent me against the nations which plunder you, for he who touches you touches the apple of His eye."

    a. A friend

    b. An enemy

    c. A servant

    d. None of the Above

ANSWERS

1. b

2. a

3. d

4. d

5. a

6. a

7. b

GRM BIBLE SCHOOL

ARK OF THE COVENANT

UNIT 14

GRM BIBLE SCHOOL

ARK OF THE COVENANT

UNIT 14

PART 1

LESSON 64

1. The _____ of the Covenant, representing the presence of God, had fallen into the hands of the Philistines (enemies of Israel).

    a. Box

    b. Ark

    c. Log

    d. None of the Above

2. We are the _____ of the Holy Spirit. All that we are, spirit, soul & body, is for the purpose of housing the Ark of the Covenant inside of us.

    a. Temple

    b. Enemy

    c. Friend

    d. None of the Above

3. This Vessel of Holiness, known as The Ark of the Covenant, was a box overlaid with _____. (Exodus 25:1-22)

    a. Silver

    b. Wood

    c. Gold

    d. Rock

4. The lid to the box (Ark) is called the Mercy _____ and represents the Throne of Glory, the throne of the living God.

    a. Seat

    b. Chair

    c. Throne

    d. Altar

5. Any leader that attempts to lead, without having met at the Throne of Glory to _____ instructions directly from the living God, cannot really lead and rule.

    a. Give

185

- b. Reject
- c. Receive
- d. Send

6. The Tablets of Testimony, the Torah, will be inside of the Ark of the Covenant, written by the _____ of God.
   - a. Angels
   - b. Word
   - c. Men
   - d. Finger

7. True or False: Inside of our heart needs to be the testimony, the Commandments of the living God, and over it needs to be the presence of the living God.
   - a. True
   - b. False

ANSWERS

1. b
2. a
3. c
4. a
5. c
6. d
7. a

GRM BIBLE SCHOOL

ARK OF THE COVENANT

UNIT 14

PART 2

Lesson 65

1. The Ark of the Covenant is the place where God houses His commandments, where Moses met with God on how to _____ the people of Israel, where the glory of the living God dwells, and where He sits on His _____ on earth.

    a. Rule, Throne

    b. Rule, People

    c. Love, Throne

    d. None of the Above

2. In 1 Samuel 5:1-5 – When the Ark is present, the idol, its _____ and its presence, is dismantled.

    a. Power

    b. Domain

    c. Rule

    d. Worshippers

3. When God's presence is there all other idols _____ to the ground.

    a. Rise

    b. Bow

    c. Fall

    d. Both A and B

4. A priesthood that both keeps and teaches the commandments of God, walking in _____ and righteousness, can handle a true revival.

    a. Unholiness

    b. Ungodliness

    c. Holiness

    d. Immorality

5. True or False: The covenant of the Lord can bring victory or it can bring defeat. God has to judge His house before He can bless His house.

    a. True

    b. False

6. In the Old Covenant, the commandments were written on _____. In the New Covenant they are written in our _____.

    a. Rock, Hands

    b. Stone, Bible

    c. Sand, Minds

    d. Stone, Hearts of flesh

7. The Tabernacle of David _____ the Ark of the Covenant. The Ark of the Covenant housed the Commandments of God. Now we are to be the Ark of the Covenant.

    a. Exposed

    b. Housed

    c. Stole

    d. Despised

ANSWERS

1. a

2. a

3. c

4. c

5. a

6. d

7. b

GRM BIBLE SCHOOL

ARK OF THE COVENANT
UNIT 14
PART 3
LESSON 66

---

1. God wants us to have a revival cry truly from the _____.
   a. Body
   b. Soul
   c. Mind
   d. Heart

2. You and I are called to be like that _____. We are called to be that place where God can place _____ Testimony.
   a. Temple, His
   b. Ark, His
   c. Tabernacle, His
   d. None of the Above

3. Our righteous doesn't come from self-effort. Our righteousness comes from a place of trust and _____.
   a. Surrender
   b. Rebellion
   c. Peace
   d. All of the Above

4. Jeremiah 31:31-34 states, "I will put my Law within them and on their _____ I will write it. They will all _____ Me."
   a. Mind, Know
   b. Forehead, See
   c. Heart, Know
   d. None of the above

5. "This book of the Law shall not depart from your _____, but you shall mediate on it day and night." (Joshua 1:8)
   a. Heart
   b. Tongue

    c. Mind
    d. Mouth
6. God did not call us to a _____ of convenience. He called us to His Kingdom.
    a. Religion
    b. Church
    c. Worship
    d. Savior
7. Revival first and foremost is a divine attack of God on _____; it breaks us down before it builds us up.
    a. Church
    b. Society
    c. Family
    d. Sinners

ANSWERS

1. d
2. b
3. a
4. c
5. d
6. a
7. b

GRM BIBLE SCHOOL

ARK OF THE COVENANT

UNIT 14

PART 4

Lesson 67

1. The Ark needs to be carried by _____ priests.
    a. All
    b. Any
    c. Disobedient
    d. Righteous

2. True or False: The presence of God can show up with unsanctified priests which will cause victory.
    a. True
    b. False

3. The first word any preacher needs to say is "_____", remove your sins off you.
    a. Repent
    b. Pray
    c. Victory
    d. All of the Above

4. The blessing we desire is that God will possess the land and that we will be totally possessed of the Holy Spirit and the _____ of God.
    a. Glory
    b. People
    c. Knowledge
    d. None of the above

5. 1 Samuel 7 describes a picture of End Time Revival: Verse 12 shows us "Ebenezer" which means the stone of help, another name for _____ the cornerstone.
    a. Moses
    b. God
    c. Yeshua
    d. Scripture

6. Elohim is bringing about a righteous _____ like Samuel, whose name means "The one who

listens to God."
- a. Disciple
- b. Pastor
- c. Church
- d. Leadership

7. For a true lasting revival we've got to have a righteous leadership, an obedient leadership, a _____ leadership.
- a. Holy
- b. Unrighteous
- c. Dishonest
- d. Lukewarm

ANSWERS

1. d
2. b
3. a
4. a
5. c
6. d
7. a

GRM BIBLE SCHOOL

Glimpses of Glory

Unit 15

GRM BIBLE SCHOOL

GLIMPSES OF GLORY

UNIT 15

PART 1

Lesson 68

1. Glimpses of what happens when you enter into the _____ of God is seen in Isaiah 6:1-8.
   a. Presence
   b. Chamber
   c. Sanctuary
   d. Glory

2. When we cry out "Woe is me", we are in _____ Cry.
   a. Repentance
   b. Painful
   c. Revival
   d. Holy

3. When you are truly washed in the blood of Yeshua, then that blood has _____ the uncleanness.
   a. Eradicated
   b. Overlooked
   c. Covered
   d. All of the above

4. When religion touches something unclean, it gives a _____, but it doesn't do the job because the people remain the same.
   a. Covering
   b. Blessing
   c. Peace
   d. None of the above

5. When the glory comes in, it immediately touches that place that has not surrendered to the living _____.
   a. Being
   b. Soul
   c. God

       d. Thing

6. He who confesses his sins and forsake them will find _____. He that hides them will be _____.
       a. Mercy, Judged
       b. Love, Justified
       c. Peace, Justified
       d. None of the Above

7. Godly sorrow brings about the fruit of _____. Every time a person truly humbles themselves, is truly sorry for their sins, God always forgives.
       a. Lawlessness
       b. Repentance
       c. Deception
       d. None of the Above

ANSWERS

1. d
2. c
3. a
4. a
5. c
6. a
7. b

GRM BIBLE SCHOOL

GLIMPSES OF GLORY

UNIT 15

PART 2

LESSON 69

1. When the glory shows up, we can fall as _____.
   a. Alive
   b. Dead
   c. Flat
   d. Rain

2. When the temple of God is opened up, it is connected with _____, the wrath of God, and the ruling and reigning of _____ on earth. (Revelation 11:15-19)
   a. Judgment, Messiah
   b. Thunder, Angels
   c. Judgment, Saints
   d. None of the Above

3. (Hebrews 9:1- Inside the Ark of the Covenant were three things: the Tablets of the _____, the rod of Aaron the priest, which budded to show his authority to the people, and the jar of _____ to remember that God is able to provide for us in every situation.
   a. Temple, Manna
   b. Testimony, Incense
   c. Testimony, Manna
   d. All of the Above

4. True or False: The Ark of the Covenant in heaven houses the commandments of God.
   a. True
   b. False

5. Matthew 22:36-40 tells us that the entire Holy Scriptures is summed up in these two commandments: "You shall love the _____ _____ _____ with all your heart, mind and strength" and "You shall love your _____ as yourself."
   a. Lord your God, Neighbor
   b. People of God, Enemies
   c. Land of Israel, Neighbor

    d. None of the Above

6. The first five commandments are equivalent to the _____ commandment Yeshua spoke about regarding relationships between man and God.
    a. Fourth
    b. Second
    c. Third
    d. First

7. The second five commandments deal with "You shall love your neighbor as _____", regarding dealings between man and _____.
    a. Family, God
    b. Everyone, God
    c. Yourself, Man
    d. None of the Above

ANSWERS

1. b
2. a
3. c
4. a
5. a
6. d
7. c

GRM BIBLE SCHOOL

GLIMPSES OF GLORY

UNIT 15

PART 3

Lesson 70

1. The temple of God will open up in heaven and the Ark of the _____ will be seen.
    a. Covenant
    b. Saints
    c. Flood
    d. None of the Above

2. True or False: We are the temple of God. Inside of us the Ark of the Covenant must be rejected.
    a. True
    b. False

3. Do not make idols, like actors or singers. If you want to follow anybody, follow _____.
    a. Pope
    b. Madonna
    c. Peter
    d. Yeshua

4. We are commanded not to take God's name in vain. The Jews are so careful about this that they don't even say the name of God – they call Him _____ (meaning "the name").
    a. HaShem
    b. Lord
    c. Baal
    d. Adonai

5. To remember the Shabbat (in Deuteronomy 5:12-14) indicates we are to be keeping it holy, which means keeping it _____ the other days, not for common use.
    a. Together with
    b. Separate from
    c. Similar to
    d. All of the above

6. The Shabbat is a day, separated from the _____, for the purposes of rest so we can spend time

with God. (Genesis 2:1-3)
   a. Beginning
   b. Law
   c. Demonic
   d. Calendar

7. One of the marks of the End Times Revival is the _____ of the Shabbat and the feasts of the Lord.
   a. Desecration
   b. Changing
   c. Dishonor
   d. Restoration

ANSWERS

1. a
2. b
3. d
4. a
5. b
6. a
7. d

GRM BIBLE SCHOOL

Treasures of The Ark

Unit 16

GRM BIBLE SCHOOL

TREASURES OF THE ARK

UNIT 16

PART 1

Lesson 71

1. We learn in Matthew 22:36-40 that "All the Law and the Prophets hang on these two commandments: You shall love _____, and You shall love your _____.
    a. God, Mammon
    b. God, Neighbor
    c. Man, God
    d. Man, Mammon

2. To keep the Shabbat holy reminds us that we are not slaves in Egypt anymore: slaves work seven days a week, the _____ people do not.
    a. Free
    b. Weak
    c. Strong
    d. All of the Above

3. Moadim means "_____."
    a. Testimonials
    b. Words
    c. Seasons
    d. A & C above

4. Those that keep the Shabbat holy will be given a better _____ than sons and daughters.
    a. Inheritance
    b. Land
    c. Name
    d. Salary

5. How do you keep the Shabbat holy in the freedom of His Holy Spirit? Separate _____ _____ from sunset Friday to sunset Saturday, worship the living God, and give Him _____.
    a. 24 hours, Time
    b. From others, Time
    c. 18 hours, Time

d. From Food, Glory

6. Leviticus 23 outlines God's moadim or testimonials; the first of these testimonials listed is _____.

   a. Sunday

   b. Shabbat

   c. Pesach

   d. Tabernacles

7. Many have taught this is for the Jews and not the Christians. In the 4th Century the Church divorced itself from its _____ foundation of faith when Constantine _____ all that was Jewish from the Church.

   a. Original, Removed

   b. Original, Retained

   c. Faulty, Accepted

   d. None of the Above

ANSWERS

1. b

2. a

3. d

4. c

5. a

6. b

7. a

GRM BIBLE SCHOOL

TREASURES OF THE ARK

UNIT 16

PART 2

Lesson 72

1. The treasures of the Ark are the Tablets of the _____.
   a. Scribes
   b. Commandments
   c. Temple
   d. None of the Above

2. The Shabbat commandment is connected with freedom from slavery. Keeping the Shabbat is an act of _____.
   a. Worship
   b. Freedom
   c. Honor
   d. None of the Above

3. Once God sets something apart for Himself, who has the right to make it unsanctified?
   a. Christians
   b. The Church
   c. Leadership
   d. Nobody

4. Daniel 7:25 states that the Beast is going to change the times and the seasons; this is a type of _____.
   a. Disobedience
   b. Evil Spirit
   c. Anti-Christ
   d. None of the Above

5. True or False: Yeshua bought our freedom, but it does not mean "the law is done away with."
   a. True
   b. False

6. Yeshua paid the price with His blood to take away our sins, so that we would love the _____ of God

and have a _____ nature, walking in obedience to that Word.

   a. Law, New
   b. People, Clean
   c. Law, Contrary
   d. Land, Peaceful

7. Leviticus 23 lists seven Feasts that are appointed times. These seven Feasts help us to see the fullness of the _____.

   a. Law
   b. Gospel
   c. Judgment
   d. All of the above

ANSWERS

1. b
2. a
3. d
4. c
5. a
6. a
7. b

GRM BIBLE SCHOOL

TREASURES OF THE ARK

UNIT 16

PART 3

Lesson 73

1. The _____ Holy Scriptures are called "sacred writings" in 2 Timothy 3:15; they are able to make you wise unto _____.
   a. Orthodox, Salvation
   b. Greek, Salvation
   c. Hebrew, Salvation
   d. Roman, Salvation

2. In the book of Galatians, Paul was dealing with the spirit of _____. We have to _____ between what is legalism and what is law.
   a. Legalism, Separate
   b. Accusation, Separate
   c. Anti-Christ, Choose
   d. None of the Above

3. In the 3 Feasts of Passover, Unleavened Bread, and First Fruits we see Yeshua was _____ on Passover, He was in the _____ during Unleavened Bread, and He _____ on First Fruits.
   a. Hanged, Grave, Woke
   b. Crucified, Grave, Rose
   c. Crucified, Grave, Woke
   d. All of the Above

4. Shavout is celebrated _____ after First Fruits and is also called Pentecost or the Feast of _____.
   a. 25 Days, Weeks
   b. 50 days, Barley
   c. 49 Days, Weeks
   d. 50 Days, Weeks

5. Fall feasts include the Feast of _____ (Rosh Hashanah), Day of _____ (Yom Kippur), and Feast of Tabernacles – also called _____.
   a. Trumpets, Atonement, Sukkot
   b. Booths, Sukkots, Atonement

    c. Trumpets, Sukkot, Shavuot

    d. Trumpets, Repentance, Sukkot

6. Every feast is a _____ of the Gospel.
    a. Denial
    b. Law
    c. Testimonial
    d. None of the Above

7. Shabbat opens up all 7 feasts; we should walk the seven feasts in the _____ of God.
    a. Joy
    b. Anointing
    c. Law
    d. Moadim

ANSWERS

1. c
2. a
3. b
4. d
5. a
6. c
7. b

GRM BIBLE SCHOOL

The Royal Commandments

Unit 17

GRM BIBLE SCHOOL

THE ROYAL COMMANDMENTS

UNIT 17

PART 1

Lesson 74

1. True or False: Yeshua divided the commandments into 2 categories: Loving the Lord (5 commandments) and Loving your neighbor (5 commandments).
   a. True
   b. False

2. Honoring your parents is an act of _____ the living God. Parents represent God on earth.
   a. Rejecting
   b. Worshipping
   c. Knowing
   d. None of the Above

3. Many people are in mental hospitals because of bitterness against their parents; _____ and release parents from all judgment.
   a. Forgive
   b. Dishonor
   c. Unite
   d. All of the Above

4. Exodus 21:17, "He who _____ his father or his mother shall surely be put to death."
   a. Honors
   b. Respects
   c. Curses
   d. Loves

5. Curses means "to dishonor," to _____.
   a. Take seriously
   b. Take lightly
   c. Cause pain
   d. Accept responsibility

6. In Genesis 9:20-27 we see one of the sons of Noah (Ham) was mocking. The other two brothers had the

_____ of God.

   a. Anointing

   b. Word

   c. Fear

   d. All of the Above

7. Proverbs 30:11-13 tells us that there is a generation that is not purified. One of the biggest things we need to be purified of is dishonoring Israel as the _____ of the faith.

   a. Mother

   b. Father

   c. Queen

   d. King

ANSWERS

1. a

2. b

3. a

4. c

5. b

6. c

7. a

GRM BIBLE SCHOOL

THE ROYAL COMMANDMENTS

UNIT 17

PART 2

Lesson 75

1. 2 Timothy 3:15-16 tells us that the Sacred Writings make Timothy wise unto salvation. At this time the New Covenant writings _____.
    a. Changed everything
    b. Did not exist yet
    c. Replaced the old
    d. None of the Above

2. We need to relate to the Old Testament as _____ Writings.
    a. Sacred
    b. Old
    c. Obsolete
    d. Strange

3. You shall love your neighbor as yourself (Commandments #6-10 in Exodus 20:13-18): You shall not _____; You shall not commit _____; You shall not _____; You shall not bear _____ witness against your neighbor; You shall not _____.
    a. Murder, Adultery, Steal, False, Covet
    b. Murder, Hate, Lust, False, Covet
    c. Murder, Lust, Steal, True, Hate
    d. Lie, Adultery, Steal, False, Covet

4. The Finger of God comes to write God's Holy Commandments in the _____ of the believer so we don't have to sin anymore.
    a. Mind
    b. Belly
    c. Hand
    d. Heart

5. Yeshua fulfills (defines and expands) The Law: He's not only talking about the act of adultery, but he's talking about the _____ of adultery.
    a. Thoughts

- b. Acts
- c. Behavior
- d. Deeds

6. 1 Corinthians 6:9-10 lists categories of unrighteousness - even if they call themselves Christians, believers, or Messianic, they _____ _____ inherit the kingdom of God.
    - a. Will likely
    - b. Will not
    - c. Will surely
    - d. All of the Above

7. God is calling a bride, one that is pure and _____. (Revelation 22:12-17)
    - a. Unclean
    - b. Holy
    - c. Unworthy
    - d. Defiled

ANSWERS

1. b
2. a
3. a
4. d
5. a
6. b
7. b

GRM BIBLE SCHOOL

Tabernacle of David Revealed

Unit 18

GRM BIBLE SCHOOL

TABERNACLE OF DAVID REVEALED

UNIT 18

PART 1

Lesson 76

1. In order for the Messiah to return, all things must be _____. We have the Holy _____ Scriptures to find out what the ancient prophets said about the restoration of all things.
    a. Restored, Hebrew
    b. Eradicated, Greek
    c. Restored, Roman
    d. All of the Above

2. The Tabernacle of David will be restored as in the days of _____.
    a. Adam
    b. Old
    c. Noah
    d. None of the Above

3. Teshuvah means "repent and _____ for restoration." Repentance is the most powerful key for _____.
    a. Return, Renewal
    b. Return, Revival
    c. Prepare, Restoration
    d. None of the Above

4. Messiah cannot return until the _____ of all things.
    a. Cancellation
    b. Destruction
    c. Restoration
    d. All of the Above

5. Yeshua will not return to Jerusalem until they say, "Baruch haba b'shem Adonai". It means:
    a. Blessed is He whose name is Adonai
    b. Blessed is He who comes in the name of the Lord
    c. Blessed is the One true Lord

d. Blessed is He who knows the Lord

6. 1 Peter 2:9 states, "But you are a chosen race, a holy Priesthood…". We are the Royal _____ standing in the gap so that the wrath of God will not destroy this world altogether.
   a. Priesthood
   b. Kings
   c. Princes
   d. Race

7. True or False: The restoration of Israel is not connected with the restoration of the Tabernacle of David.
   a. True
   b. False

ANSWERS

1. a
2. b
3. b
4. c
5. b
6. a
7. b

GRM BIBLE SCHOOL

TABERNACLE OF DAVID REVEALED

UNIT 18
PART 2

LESSON 77

---

1. True or False: Unless Israel is restored, Yeshua will not return.
    a. True
    b. False

2. "For _____ sake I will not keep silent, and for Jerusalem's sake I will not keep quiet, Until her righteous goes forth like brightness, her salvation like a torch that is burning." (Isaiah 62:1)
    a. Rome's
    b. Adonai's
    c. Zion's
    d. Salvation's

3. We are to abstain from idolatry and immorality which includes some_____ commandments. Whatever we eat needs to be sanctified by two things: The _____ and prayer.
    a. Dietary, Word
    b. Other, Word
    c. Legalistic, Law
    d. Holy, Word

4. Acts Chapter 3 directs us to the ancient _____. Acts Chapter 15 directs us to the _____ of Moses.
    a. Laws, Words
    b. Prophets, Law
    c. Priesthood, Words
    d. None of the Above

5. Restoration of the Tabernacle of David is restoration of _____.
    a. Intimacy
    b. Religion
    c. Law
    d. Obedience

6. Consecrate yourselves so you can _____ the Ark to the place I have prepared for it, just as David sanctified a priesthood and prepared a place (Jerusalem).
   a. Move
   b. Carry
   c. Consecrate
   d. None of the Above

7. Restoration of the Tabernacle of David represents the _____ Covenant, which needs to be written in our hearts.
   a. Abrahamic
   b. Old
   c. Salt
   d. New

ANSWERS

1. a
2. c
3. a
4. b
5. a
6. b
7. d

GRM BIBLE SCHOOL

TABERNACLE OF DAVID REVEALED

UNIT 18

PART 3

LESSON 78

1. Restoration of the Tabernacle of David is directly related to the restoration of _____.
   a. Judaism
   b. Nations
   c. Christianity
   d. Israel

2. 1 Chronicles 16:37 states that priests are to minister before the Ark _____.
   a. Daily
   b. On Shabbat
   c. Continually
   d. Diligently

3. Relevance for Today – Yeshua has called you and I to be a _____ sacrifice, to let the fire burn continually inside of us, bringing about holy praise and worship in spirit and in truth.
   a. Living
   b. Boastful
   c. Burning
   d. Fleshly

4. The Spirit and fire that comes into believers burns the _____ out of our lives.
   a. Chaff and righteousness
   b. Chaff and sin
   c. Hope and joy
   d. None of the Above

5. During Shavuot the _____ was given. On the same date the _____ of God is given.
   a. Torah, Word
   b. Torah, Commandments
   c. Torah, Laws
   d. Torah, Spirit

6. True or False: Without the fire of God inside of us we cannot have the fullness of the Tabernacle of David restored.
    a. True
    b. False

7. The fire of God inside of us will burn every _____ for lust and sin, causing us to _____ the laws and commandments of God.
    a. Desire, Reject
    b. Need, Break
    c. Reason, Hate
    d. Desire, Love

ANSWERS

1. d
2. c
3. a
4. b
5. d
6. a
7. d

GRM BIBLE SCHOOL

TABERNACLE OF DAVID REVEALED

UNIT 18

PART 4

Lesson 79

1. Key for world revival is that the Church will be restored back to the original _____ foundations.
   a. Hebrew
   b. Religious
   c. Roman
   d. Greek

2. True or False: He needs to sanctify us by the truth, Jew and Gentile, so that the world may believe that the Father sent the Son. (John 17:17)
   a. True
   b. False

3. There is a unity of Jew and Gentile, based on the original Gospel preached from _____ to the nations.
   a. Rome
   b. United States of America
   c. Zion
   d. Mt. Sinai

4. David means well: as he is praising God they were carrying the Ark on a new cart in a new way. It brought _____ to the Levite because of his irreverence. (2 Samuel 6:1-6)
   a. Curses
   b. Death
   c. Sickness
   d. None of the Above

5. The Church has forgotten that it is grafted into the _____ Tree and not the Christmas tree (symbol of a pagan feast). It has forgotten the basic foundations of faith.
   a. Olive
   b. Pine
   c. Sycamore
   d. Palm

6. The threshing floor is the place of separation between wheat and chaff. Matthew 3:11-12 tells us, "He will baptize us in the Holy Spirit and fire, and He will_____ off the chaff.
   a. Winnow
   b. Burn
   c. Blow
   d. All of the above

7. We should be like those in Ezekiel 44: They do everything in the Spirit. They are a constant living sacrifice, teaching the difference between the _____ and profane, keeping the laws and the statutes and all the _____ feasts.
   a. Good, Biblical
   b. Evil, Holy
   c. Holy, Appointed
   d. Holy, Pagan

ANSWERS

1. a
2. a
3. c
4. b
5. a
6. b
7. c

GRM BIBLE SCHOOL

Women in Ministry

Unit 19

GRM BIBLE SCHOOL

WOMEN IN MINISTRY

UNIT 19

PART 1

Lesson 80

1. Rabbi Baruch wanted to be a _____ of women in Ministry before he met Archbishop Dominiquae.
    a. Supporter
    b. Lover
    c. Persecutor
    d. Counselor

2. The first preacher of the resurrection of Yeshua was:
    a. A man
    b. A woman
    c. One of the apostles
    d. The high priest

3. The ones financing Yeshua's ministry were_____.
    a. His disciples
    b. Priests
    c. Women
    d. The tax collectors

4. Priscilla was the _____ of a house church.
    a. Leader
    b. Deacon
    c. House cleaner
    d. Door keeper

5. Priscilla _____ to a man called Apollos.
    a. Made lunch
    b. Taught doctrine
    c. Showed the way
    d. Brought dishonor

6. Philip, the proclaimer of Good News, who was one of the seven, had 4 virgin daughters who _____ Acts 21:8-9
   a. Prophesied
   b. Danced
   c. Made dresses
   d. Were lunatics

7. In Greek, the adjective does not change depending on whether you are talking to a man or a woman.
   a. True
   b. False

ANSWERS

1. c
2. b
3. c
4. a
5. b
6. a
7. a

GRM BIBLE SCHOOL

WOMEN IN MINISTRY

UNIT 19

PART 2

Lesson 81

---

1. Who is the ruling deacon of the Church? (Romans 16:1)
   a. The pastor
   b. The evangelist
   c. The church servant
   d. The prophet

2. (Romans 16:7) In the original Greek, the name of the apostle is Junia (female name).
   a. True
   b. False

3. With an understanding of Greek and Church history you will get the truth of the Scriptures in the New Covenant.
   a. True
   b. False

4. In 1 Corinthians Chapter 14 Paul is restoring _____ to the Church.
   a. Prophecy
   b. Torah
   c. Order
   d. Truth

5. The Greek word laleo means (1 Corinthians 14:34):
   a. Speak
   b. Boast
   c. Call out to somebody across the room
   d. All of the above

6. (1 Timothy 2:8-10) What women was Paul referring to as those having braided hair, gold and pearls?
   a. Married women
   b. Virgins
   c. Elderly women

    d. Temple prostitutes that have recently been saved

7. 1 Timothy 2:12 states, "I do not allow a woman to teach or exercise authority (Greek: authenteo) over a man, but to be quiet." Is this referring to women (ex-prostitutes) using their sexuality to make men do what they want, by manipulating them?

    a. True

    b. False

ANSWERS

1. a
2. a
3. a
4. c
5. d
6. d
7. a

GRM BIBLE SCHOOL

HEBREW SCRIPTURES RESTORED

Reading Schedule

1. The Key of Abraham
2. The MAP Revolution
3. The Bible Cure for Africa and the Nations
4. The Woman Factor

BOOK 1

The Key of Abraham

---

1. The Key of Abraham key (Genesis 12:3 has the power to open the entire world for the end-time revival. And whoever will be willing to receive this key and pay the price and carry it and use it, it will be a _____ for revival in churches, cities, regions and nations.
    a. Point of Contact
    b. Point of Reference
    c. Center of Excellence
    d. None of the above

2. Matthew 16:15-19 - When we receive the revelation knowledge of Messiah Yeshua of His true Jewish identity just like Apostle Peter, we will have the power and the authority to shut down every operation of demonic activities being released from _____ in our nations because we are now standing on a solid ROCK.
    a. Doors of Churches
    b. Gates of Hell
    c. Gates of Religion
    d. Gates of Heaven

3. The Gates of Hell are evident in many places and they are the point of contact with the demonic world. Such places include and are not limited to: _____.
    a. Abortion Clinics

b. Witches Covens

   c. Masonic Lodges

   d. All of the above

4. _____ is the City of the Great King and is the strongest "Portal of Heaven." She is called the "Throne of the Lord" established here on earth. (Jeremiah 3:17)

   a. Rome

   b. Vatican City

   c. Jerusalem

   d. Greece

5. True or False: One of the practical things you can do in order to close the Gates of Hell and open the Portal of Heaven is to "Break your vow with the Council of Nicaea, with Constantine, and Martin Luther's erroneous teachings against the Jews and against the Law of God."

   a. True

   b. False

6. Yahveh responded to Yeshua, who was by far the most meaningful "Contact Point" on earth. He was the _____ sacrifice that opened up the Portal of Heaven.

   a. Ordinary

   b. Extravagant

   c. Blessed

   d. None of the Above

7. The sins of the church towards the Covenant People, the Jews, have caused a deadly plague to be running through the church to this day. Historically this plague has brought death to millions of Jews and has caused millions of Christians to be broken off the Olive Tree (Romans 11:19). And because of this, there is no _____ nation in sight.

   a. Sheep

   b. Goat

   c. Wolf

   d. All of the Above

8. True or False: The Jews are like an electric socket. They are the point of contact for Yahveh (Genesis 12:3) to release His Light and Power to bless all mankind, families, tribes and nations of the earth.

   a. False

   b. True

9. Rahab the prostitute, Ruth of the Moabites (who were cursed for ten generations), and Cornelius the Roman Centurion are great biblical examples of _____ into the Key of Abraham and the Jewish Roots of Faith – these two women are named in the Royal Lineage of Yeshua (Matthew 1).

   a. Right Plugging

   b. Wrong Plugging

   c. Both A & B

d. None of the Above

10. Sacrificial and Extravagant giving to the _____ will reverse curses and release "Protection, Favor, Blessings, and Family Salvation and Restoration" (that seems unattainable) because they are the Contact Points for all nations, tribes and tongues.

    a. Local Church Pastors

    b. Jewish People

    c. Mega Religious Concerts

    d. Religious Leaders

    ANSWERS

    1. a   2. b   3. d   4. c   5. a   6. b   7. a   8. b   9. a   10. b

GRM BIBLE SCHOOL

BOOK 2

The MAP Revolution

---

1. The true church of Yahveh is based on The Holy Scriptures as revealed to Israel, with all of God's laws and commandments and His instructions on how to live for His Glory on this earth. This is known as Yahveh's _____ for the Church.
    a. Blueprint
    b. Watermark
    c. Both A & B
    d. None of the Above

2. Without the Spirit of Truth, there is no end time _____. Without the Spirit of Truth, there is no real _____ between the Jews and the Gentile. Without the Spirit of Truth, there is no _____ in the Body of the Messiah.
    a. Revival, Unity, Growth
    b. Cleansing, Unity, Love
    c. Rapture, Blood, Growth
    d. None of the Above

3. The MAP Movement is a _____ and its primary purpose is _____ - based upon Acts 3:19-21.
    a. Revival, Reformation
    b. Revolution, Restoration
    c. Reformation, Revival
    d. None of the Above

4. True or False: In Hebrew the word "Kad-esh" means "Vessel of Fire" and it describes the function of the Kad-Esh MAP Ministry. MAP stands for "Messianic Apostolic Prophetic" which is the description of the entire movement.
    a. True
    b. False

5. The purpose of many world revolutions (like the American Revolution) is to break free from the oppression and suppression of the tyrants and dictators that were enslaving the people. So too is our "spiritual revolution". By submitting to Yahveh, we are to put up spiritual resistance (James 4:7) against the powers of _____ and to break free from demonically inspired laws and ideologies.
    a. Darkness
    b. Heavens

c. Earth

   d. None of the above

6. Yeshua was a revolutionary: He did not come to abolish the law or the prophets (Matthew 5:17). He did not come to establish a _____ system or to divide us up into many denominations. Instead He came to establish the Law and to call us to the Kingdom and to obedience to His Father's Commandments.

   a. Church

   b. Religious

   c. World

   d. None of the Above

7. True or False: The error of Replacement Theology is like a cancer in the Church today. And some of its fruits are: Divorce from the original Jewish Roots Foundation, Lack of Fear of God, Mixture of Paganism and Babylonian worship, Loss of honor and obedience to God's Commandments.

   a. True

   b. False

8. The church has failed the Great Commission which is to go into the whole world and make "disciples of all nations" (Matthew 28:19). But instead, she has done it wrongly and has used her authority (Council of Nicaea mandate) to teach the nations to hate Yahveh's _____ and forget His _____.

   a. Miracles, Commandments

   b. Laws, Commandments

   c. Neither A nor B

   d. All of the Above

9. Everything that was changed, including the establishment of the Tree of _____ during the Council of Nicaea, needs to be completely reversed and uprooted from the body of the Messiah and should not be allowed to exist and grow any further.

   a. Israel

   b. Rome

   c. Germany

   d. Christianity

10. The Doctrinal Errors of the Council of Nicaea set out in the "Letter of Constantine" needs to be revoked in its entirety: Yahveh does not call us to seek out a universally _____ way to worship Him, but to complete obedience to His Commandments and Moadims.

    a. Rejected

    b. Uniform

    c. Convenient

    d. None of the Above.

ANSWERS

1. a   2. a   3. b   4. a   5. a   6. b   7. a   8. b   9. d   10. c

GRM BIBLE SCHOOL

BOOK 3

THE BIBLE CURE FOR AFRICA AND THE NATIONS

---

1. True or False: History tells us that the relationship with Africa and Israel in the last 40 years has been problematic.
   a. True
   b. False

2. The blessing or the _____ on EVERY nation and ethnic group (based on Gen. 12:3) depends on one factor: how the nations have treated Israel and the Jewish people.
   a. Prosperity
   b. Curse
   c. Inheritance
   d. Promise

3. Africa needs a cure from _____ and return to the original Gospel made in Zion, preached by 12 Jewish Apostles of the Lamb 2000 years ago.
   a. European Christianity
   b. Diseases
   c. Famine
   d. None of the above

4. The entire modern day "political conflict" over Israel is nothing but a "Biblical conflict" between those nations that _____ Israel's right to settle in the whole land promised to Abraham and between those nations that are opposing the will of God almighty – they find themselves His enemy.
   a. Hate
   b. Oppose
   c. Support
   d. All of the above

5. After years of friendship with African leaders (until the Six Day War in June 1967), Africans became increasingly critical of Israel and supportive of the _____ Cause, until most had renounced their friendship with Israel & broken off diplomatic relations by the Yom Kippur War (Oct. 1973).
   a. American
   b. Arab
   c. Egyptian
   d. European

6. The issue of _____ is the KEY issue for the overturning of the situation in Africa – since they have repaid good with evil concerning Israel. (Prov. 17:13)
   a. Holiness
   b. Politics
   c. Restitution
   d. Trade

7. Africa's church leaders must repent from Replacement Theology and get grafted into the _____ with Israel, in order to catapult its nations out of the curse.
   a. United Nations
   b. Olive Tree
   c. Promised Land
   d. Economy

8. Earthquakes, hurricanes and floods are some of the catastrophes directly related to the attempts to side with Palestinians & _____ the land of Israel. All of Africa has also experienced poverty, disease and humiliation.
   a. Divide
   b. Bless
   c. Purchase
   d. All of the above

9. Steps for Africans to take are described in Zephaniah 3:8-11 – worshippers "from beyond the rivers of _____ will bring offerings" as an act of worship and restitution.
   a. Kenya
   b. Ethiopia
   c. Israel
   d. Egypt

10. The First Council of Nicea of 325 AD contains many lies and doctrinal _____ seeking to separate believers from the "detestable company of the Jew".
    a. Ideas
    b. Decisions
    c. Errors
    d. None of the above

ANSWERS

1. a   2. b   3. a   4. c   5. b   6. c   7. b   8. a   9. b   10. c

GRM BIBLE SCHOOL

BOOK 4

THE WOMAN FACTOR

---

1. True or False: Before the fall of Adam in the Garden of Eden, Adam was created both "male and female" and given the same authority and mandate to rule over the earth and to be fruitful and multiply (Genesis 1:26-27). But the "female Adam" fell from her position of authority the moment she ate the forbidden fruit.

    a. True

    b. False

2. Since Yeshua came and died on the cross, the curse of breaking the commandments of Elohim God is now broken (Galatians 3:13); male and female exist as co-equal partners of the gift of life, both with _____ to rule and reign to advance the Kingdom of Elohim God.

    a. Hope

    b. Children

    c. Identity

    d. Authority

3. Men cannot allow women to be preachers and teachers of the word in the church today as a result of the_____ and teachings of the scripture in Ephesians 5:22 where it says, "Wives, submit to your husbands as to the Lord."

    a. Erroneous Understanding

    b. Correct Understanding

    c. Correct Interpretation

    d. None of the Above

4. Yahveh is not a respecter of persons as we see in the stories of Rebecca (Genesis 27), Deborah (Judges 5), Abigail (2 Samuel 2) and Huldah (2 Kings 2) in the Bible. Therefore, in this end times, it is now _____ for mothers and mighty women in the body of Messiah Yeshua to arise in their leadership offices so that the church can have victory against the enemy.

    a. No Time

    b. Unnecessary

    c. High Time

    d. Too late

5. Many times Yahveh reveals His plans to women (with the likes of Rebecca and Abigail, for example, in the Bible) and not their husbands (men). But because many men are full of _____, they will not pay attention or listen to women that are wiser than they.

    a. Pride

b. Shame

   c. Blame

   d. Hate

6. Jezebel is a destructive spirit. Anyone that possess the spirit of Jezebel:

   a. Hates YHVH and His Anointing

   b. Hates, Persecutes, Defames and Murders YHVH's Prophets

   c. Influences the people towards idolatry and immorality

   d. Connives, Intimidates and Manipulates until it gets its way at whatever cost

   e. All of the Above.

7. True or False. In the New Testament (because of the translators' biasness) women leaders are not recognized properly or given prominence in the scriptures for their respective roles they played in spreading the Gospel with the Apostles.

   a. True

   b. False

8. The Apostle Paul recognized Phoebe as a woman leader with _____ in her local church: she was a Senior Pastor and a Deacon of her ministry (Romans 16:1-2) which associated with Paul.

   a. Strength

   b. Might

   c. Authority

   d. None of the above

9. If the context of 1 Corinthians 11:15-16 and 1 Corinthians 14:34-36 are understood correctly, one would come to clearly know that the purpose was to _____ the congregation from outside influences.

   a. Protect

   b. Discredit

   c. Scold

   d. None of the above

10. The woman at the well (John 4), Mary Magdalene (John 20), Pastor Phoebe (Romans 16:1) Pastor Lydia (Acts 16:11-40) are great examples of women in Ministry, showing that YHVH does not _____ between men and women when He calls to His Service.

    a. Favor

    b. Choose

    c. Select

    d. Discriminate

ANSWERS

1. a   2. d   3. a   4. c   5. a   6. e   7. a   8. c   9. a   10. d

GRM BIBLE SCHOOL

HEBREW SCRIPTURES RESTORED

Term Paper

INSTRUCTIONS

In four pages to ten pages, discuss what you have learned through Lessons 56-81 and the four books by Archbishop Dominiquae Bierman. Make sure to include the following points:

1. Trace the lifestyles of the enemies of God. Why were they enemies? What did they all have in common?

2. How was Josiah different? What is it that made him repent?

3. The Ark of the Covenant inside of God's people.

4. The Ten Commandments. How serious is God about His Commandments?

5. Discuss about laws other than the Ten Commandments such as dietary laws, God's *Moadim*, laws of purity, and others?

6. What is righteous priesthood, or righteous leadership, and how is it important.

Make sure to cite all references. Biblical references need book, chapter, and verse. For example: Isaiah 53:4-6. Book references for Archbishop's books need title and page number. Use quotation marks for direct quotes. Other material cite appropriately.

FORMAT

- Double spaced with 12pt font
- Your Name
- Title as, "Hebrew Scriptures Restored Term Paper"
- Summary: This is a one paragraph summary of your term paper.
- Main Section: Make sure it has a logical flow with an introduction, main body, and conclusion.
- Practical Application: This is a separate section at the end. Include what have you learned and how you can use this information or how it can be applied in these end times. Include any new insights you may have.

GRM BIBLE SCHOOL
Appendix A – The Ten Commandments

The Ten Commandments can be found in Exodus 20:1-17 and in Deuteronomy 5:6-21. There are differences in dividing them between Roman Catholic, Lutheran, Anglican, Protestant, Orthodox, or Jewish traditions. Within the accepted ten, there are actually about 14 or 15 distinct commandments. The division here is according to Jewish tradition.

It must be noted here that these are not the only commandments found in the Holy Scriptures. When the laws, commandments, statutes, and precepts of God are referred to, all the commandments in scripture are included. Many people are afraid of being "put under the law" and being restricted.

Rather than restrict, the law frees us and gives structure to our lives. Contrary to the interpretation of Replacement Theology, Yeshua did not come to "free" us from the laws of God and often His interpretation was stricter as can be noted in the commentary on commandments 6 and 7 below. You can also read Matthew 5:21-48.

The First Commandment

"I am the LORD your God who brought you out of the land of Egypt, from the house of slavery. You shall have no other gods before Me."

This commandment is to believe in the existence of God and His influence on events in the world, and that the goal of the redemption from Egypt was to become His servants. It prohibits belief in or worship of any additional deities.

The Second Commandment

"You shall not make for yourself an idol, or any likeness of what is in heaven above or on the earth beneath or in the water under the earth. You shall not worship them or serve them."

This prohibits the construction or fashioning of "idols" in the likeness of created things (beasts, fish, birds, people), or imaginary things, and worshipping them.

The Third Commandment

"You shall not take the name of YHVH your Elohim (God) in vain..."

This commandment is to never take the name of YHVH in vain, speak lightly in His name, make insincere promises in His name, or bringing reproach upon his Holy Name because of improper or sinful behavior.

The Fourth Commandment

"Remember the Shabbat and keep it holy. (the version in Deuteronomy reads "observe the Shabbat") Six days you shall labor and do all your work, but the seventh day is a Shabbat of YHVH your Elohim; in it you shall not do any work, you or your son or your daughter, your male or your female servant…"

The seventh day of the week is termed Shabbat and is holy. The scripture is very clear that we are not to work for our sustenance on Shabbat.

The Fifth Commandment

"Honor your father and your mother, that your days may be prolonged… "

The obligation to honor one's parents is an obligation owed to Elohim (God) and fulfills this obligation through actions towards one's parents. It is important to note that it does not say to honor you father and your mother only if they deserve it. This is such an important point that in other areas of Torah a sentence of death could be carried out for dishonoring one's parents.

The Sixth Commandment

"You shall not murder."

This is not a commandment against killing but against murder. Justified killing such as in war or self-defense is permitted. Yeshua said, "You have heard that the ancients were told, 'You shall not commit murder' and 'Whoever commits murder shall be liable to the court.' "But I say to you that everyone who is angry with his brother shall be guilty before the court." (Matthew 5:22-23)

The Seventh Commandment

"You shall not commit adultery."

Any sex by a married person other than with their partner is adultery. This includes masturbation, pornography, or anything else that is not strictly with the marriage partner. Yeshua said, "You have heard that it was said, You shall not commit adultery; but I say to you that everyone who looks at a woman with lust for her has already committed adultery with her in his heart." (Matthew 5:27-28)

The Eighth Commandment

"You shall not steal."

According to some commentators this can also be taken as "You shall not kidnap." It includes taking or "kidnapping" anything that does not legally belong to you.

The Ninth Commandment

"You shall not bear false witness against your neighbor."

You shall not lie about your neighbor (bringing bad reputation on him) or to your neighbor or misleading him/her. "Outside are the dogs and the sorcerers and the immoral persons and the murderers and the idolaters, and everyone who loves and practices lying." (Revelation 22:15)

The Tenth Commandment

"You shall not covet your neighbor's house … or anything that belongs to your neighbor"

It is forbidden to desire and plan how one may obtain that which Elohim-God has given to another. Throughout scripture coveting is condemned except in one area where it says we are to covet the best gifts of the Holy Spirit. (1 Corinthians 12:31)

OTHER LAWS AND COMMANDMENTS

There are many other commandments in the Holy Scriptures. The following are by no means all of God's commandments and are listed here for your reference.

Dietary Laws	Deuteronomy 14 & Leviticus 11
The Greatest Commandment	Deuteronomy 6:4-9
Gods Moadim (appointed times)	Deuteronomy 16 & Leviticus 23
Moral Laws	Leviticus 18
Social Laws	Leviticus 19
Some of Yeshua's Commandments	Matthew 5-8

Appendix B: For Further Studies

To study further, please go to www.grmbibleschool.com/course-overview/, or email us at info@grmbibleschool.com to be given further steps. Our school offers the following educational degrees:

- Bachelors of Arts in Hebrew Studies
- Masters of Divinity in Hebrew Studies
- Ph.D. in Religious Philosophy

Appendix C: Graduation & Ordination

GRADUATION

Upon completion of GRM Bible School Levels 1-3, students will get an official GRM Israeli Bible School Graduation Certificate. We invite all graduates to attend a special graduation ceremony in Jerusalem during our annual Sukkot Tour of Israel (www.zionsgospel.com/tours-and-events/).

ORDINATION

Graduates may receive ordination upon request to start a ministry or a MAP (Messianic, Apostolic, Prophetic) lighthouse. They must be graduates in GRM Israeli Bible School and have attended one full tour of Israel with Kad-Esh MAP Ministries.

All ordinations will be contingent on confirmation by the Holy Spirit, and will only take place in Israel. Those chosen to be ordained will be sent into the nations from Jerusalem, fulfilling the prophecy of Isaiah: "For the law will go forth from Zion and the Word of the Lord from Jerusalem." – Isaiah 2:3